MW00957412

IELTS WRITING TASK 1+2

The Ultimate Guide With Practice To Get A Target Band Score Of 8.0+ In 10 Minutes A Day

RACHEL MITCHELL

ISBN: 9781549683381

TABLE OF CONTENT

INTRODUCTION

Thank you and congratulate you for purchasing the book *"IELTS Academic Writing Task 1 + 2: The Ultimate Guide with Practice to Get a Target Band Score of 8.0+ In 10 Minutes a Day."*

This book is well designed and written by an experienced native teacher from the USA who has been teaching IELTS for over 10 years. She really is the expert in training IELTS for students at each level. In this book, she will provide you all proven formulas, tips, strategies, explanations, structures, task 1 + Task 2 language, vocabulary, reports and model essays to help you easily achieve an 8.0+ in the IELTS Writing section, even if your English is not excellent. This book will also walk you through step-by-step on how to develop your well-organised answers for the Task 1 + Task 2 Writing; clearly explains the different types of questions that are asked for Task 1 + Task 2; provide you step-by-step instructions on how to write each type of report and essay excellently.

As the author of this book, Rachel Mitchell believes that this book will be an indispensable reference and trusted guide for you who may want to maximize your band score in IELTS Academic Task 1 + Task 2 Writing. Once you read this book, I guarantee you that you will have learned an extraordinarily wide range of useful, and practical IELTS WRITNG strategies and formulas that will help you become a successful IELTS taker as well as you will even become a successful English user in work and in life within a short period of time only.

Take action today and start getting better scores tomorrow!

Thank you again for purchasing this book, and I hope you enjoy it.

IELTS WRITING INTRODUCTION

The IELTS Academic Writing lasts for 60 minutes (an hour). In the 1 hour, you have to complete 2 tasks, task 1 is a report, and task 2 is an essay. It is suggested that you should spend about 20 minutes on task 1 and about 40 minutes on task 2. In the IELTS Academic Writing task 1, you are required to write at least 150 words (10 to 15 sentences) and 220 words maximum. On the other hand, in the IELTS Academic Writing task 2, you are required to write at least 250 words (20 to 25 sentences) and 300 words maximum. Writing task 1 accounts for 1/3 while writing task 2 accounts for 2/3 of your total writing score.

In the IELTS Writing test, you need to use academic language. It's not informal language (it's not an email to your friend). We need to use academic language.

IELTS WRITING TASK 1

What are they asking you to do in a report?

They're asking you to *describe the main points* of the diagram. When I say *"describe"*, I mean you will tell them *what the diagram looks like*? For example, I have a diagram that shows fast food consumption, I simply need to describe *that fast food consumption has increased/ has grown/ has risen*; I don't need to say *"fast food consumption has risen because fast food is delicious and affordable"* **No**, you don't need to explain, ok?. Explaining is what you are going to do essays in task 2 writing. Therefore, in task 1 writing, your job is to *describe the main points of a diagram.*

What is a diagram? You might be asking. That's a good question. These are all examples of diagrams.

Diagrams are pictures that convey information, usually numbers. This is a type of a diagram called <u>flow chart</u>, and a flow chart shows us how to do something, a method to do something.

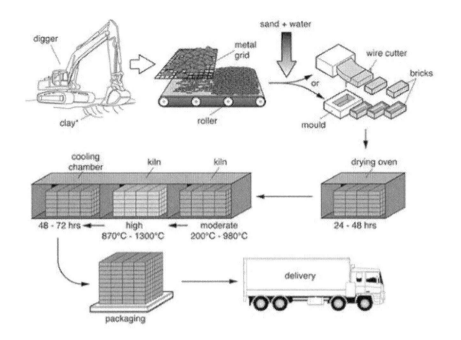

Here, this is a type of a diagram called line chart or a line graph. It shows changes over time/ over a period of time.

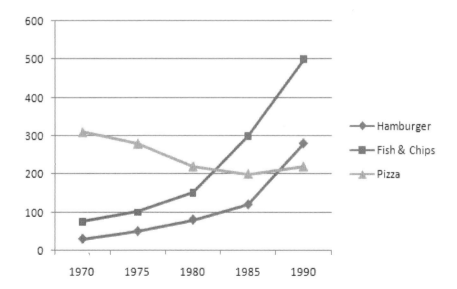

And here is a type of diagram called <u>a table</u>. You're very familiar with tables. Every time you go to restaurants, every time you're looking at a menu, you are looking at the table. Every time you go to the KFC, you're looking at a table. Every time you go to the airport, and you see the arrival time, the departure time, you're looking at a table. These are very common in our lives.

Selected leisure activities Participation rates in the four weeks before the interview (by age)			
Leisure activities	% of age group		
	16-19	25-29	60-69
Watching TV / DVDs	99	99	99
Visiting / entertaining friends / relations	98	98	95
Listening to music	98	93	65
Reading books	63	64	66
DIY	25	50	38
Gardening	15	35	61
Dressmaking/Needlework/Knitting	9	14	27

Another type of a diagram is a <u>pie chart</u>. We use a pie chart to show a percentage out of 100. That's why we use a pie chart.

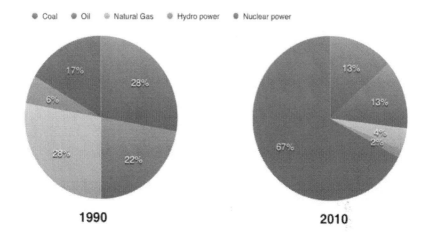

Percentage of electricity production by fuel source in France in 1990 and 2010

● Coal ● Oil ● Natural Gas ● Hydro power ● Nuclear power

1990

2010

And right here is a column graph, or a bar graph. This one shows percentages but over a period of time.

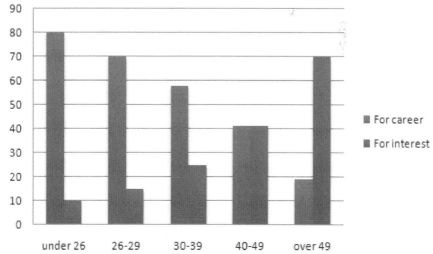

Reasons for study according to age of student

■ For career
■ For interest

So, what we're looking at in task 1 writing is all these types of diagrams including maps.

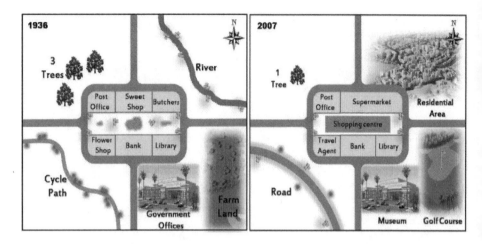

These are all types of diagrams that you need to be familiar with so you can describe them in task 1 writing.

All right, when it comes to **task 1 writing**, there are a few rules you need to pay your attention to. First of all, task 1 requires 150 words minimum. If you write <u>fewer than 150 words</u>, you're going to <u>face a penalty</u>. Therefore, you should try to write at least 150 words. I will tell you that <u>it will be difficult for you to get a high score if you're only writing 150 words</u>. You probably will need to write 200 or 210 words to get a high score (7.5 - 8.0).

For **task 2 writing**, <u>it's larger</u>. It needs 250 words minimum, and the essay is worth 2/3 of your score. It's worth twice of task 1. Therefore, I would like to tell you that you should write task 2 first and spend 40 minutes on it.

Now, we will focus on task 1 writing, we will be describing different kinds of diagrams.

How are they marking you? How are they assessing you? How are they giving you a score in task 1 writing?

Let's look at the IELTS writing task 1 band score descriptors below:

IELTS TASK 1 Writing band descriptors (public version)

Band	Task Achievement	Coherence and Cohesion	Lexical Resource	Grammatical Range and Accuracy
9	• fully satisfies all the requirements of the task • clearly presents a fully developed response	• uses cohesion in such a way that it attracts no attention • skilfully manages paragraphing	• uses a wide range of vocabulary with very natural and sophisticated control of lexical features; rare minor errors occur only as 'slips'	• uses a wide range of structures with full flexibility and accuracy; rare minor errors occur only as 'slips'
8	• covers all requirements of the task sufficiently • presents, highlights and illustrates key features/bullet points clearly and appropriately	• sequences information and ideas logically • manages all aspects of cohesion well • uses paragraphing sufficiently and appropriately	• uses a wide range of vocabulary fluently and flexibly to convey precise meanings • skilfully uses uncommon lexical items but there may be occasional inaccuracies in word choice and collocation • produces rare errors in spelling and/or word formation	• uses a wide range of structures • the majority of sentences are error-free • makes only very occasional errors or inappropriacies
7	• covers the requirements of the task • (Academic) presents a clear overview of main trends, differences or stages • (General Training) presents a clear purpose, with the tone consistent and appropriate • clearly presents and highlights key features/bullet points but could be more fully extended	• logically organises information and ideas; there is clear progression throughout • uses a range of cohesive devices appropriately although there may be some under-/over-use	• uses a sufficient range of vocabulary to allow some flexibility and precision • uses less common lexical items with some awareness of style and collocation • may produce occasional errors in word choice, spelling and/or word formation	• uses a variety of complex structures • produces frequent error-free sentences • has good control of grammar and punctuation but may make a few errors
6	• addresses the requirements of the task • (Academic) presents an overview with information appropriately selected • (General Training) presents a purpose that is generally clear; there may be inconsistencies in tone • presents and adequately highlights key features/bullet points but details may be irrelevant, inappropriate or inaccurate	• arranges information and ideas coherently and there is a clear overall progression • uses cohesive devices effectively, but cohesion within and/or between sentences may be faulty or mechanical • may not always use referencing clearly or appropriately	• uses an adequate range of vocabulary for the task • attempts to use less common vocabulary but with some inaccuracy • makes some errors in spelling and/or word formation, but they do not impede communication	• uses a mix of simple and complex sentence forms • makes some errors in grammar and punctuation but they rarely reduce communication

5	• generally addresses the task; the format may be inappropriate in places • (Academic) recounts detail mechanically with no clear overview; there may be no data to support the description • (General Training) may present a purpose for the letter that is unclear at times; the tone may be variable and sometimes inappropriate • presents, but inadequately covers, key features/bullet points; there may be a tendency to focus on detail	• presents information with some organisation but there may be a lack of overall progression • makes inadequate, inaccurate or over-use of cohesive devices • may be repetitive because of lack of referencing and substitution	• uses a limited range of vocabulary, but this is minimally adequate for the task • may make noticeable errors in spelling and/or word formation that may cause some difficulty for the reader	• uses only a limited range of structures • attempts complex sentences but these tend to be less accurate than simple sentences • may make frequent grammatical errors and punctuation may be faulty; errors can cause some difficulty for the reader
4	• attempts to address the task but does not cover all key features/bullet points; the format may be inappropriate • (General Training) fails to clearly explain the purpose of the letter; the tone may be inappropriate • may confuse key features/bullet points with detail; parts may be unclear, irrelevant, repetitive or inaccurate	• presents information and ideas but these are not arranged coherently and there is no clear progression in the response • uses some basic cohesive devices but these may be inaccurate or repetitive	• uses only basic vocabulary which may be used repetitively or which may be inappropriate for the task • has limited control of word formation and/or spelling; • errors may cause strain for the reader	• uses only a very limited range of structures with only rare use of subordinate clauses • some structures are accurate but errors predominate, and punctuation is often faulty
3	• fails to address the task, which may have been completely misunderstood • presents limited ideas which may be largely irrelevant/repetitive	• does not organise ideas logically • may use a very limited range of cohesive devices, and those used may not indicate a logical relationship between ideas	• uses only a very limited range of words and expressions with very limited control of word formation and/or spelling • errors may severely distort the message	• attempts sentence forms but errors in grammar and punctuation predominate and distort the meaning
2	• answer is barely related to the task	• has very little control of organisational features	• uses an extremely limited range of vocabulary; essentially no control of word formation and/or spelling	• cannot use sentence forms except in memorised phrases
1	• answer is completely unrelated to the task	• fails to communicate any message	• can only use a few isolated words	• cannot use sentence forms at all
0	• does not attend • does not attempt the task in any way • writes a totally memorised response			

I want you to know that IELTS <u>keeps their scoring very secretive</u>. IELTS does not tell you how they score your writing. The information that we have about how they score our writing is we have got pieces of information from people over the years. They think that we all know about IELTS. Let's talk something that you need to know about how they mark your test.

First of all, the IELTS examiner will mark your test according to four categories:

1. Task Achievement (25%)
2. Coherence and Cohesion (25%)
3. Lexical Resource (25%)
4. Grammatical Range and Accuracy (25%)

Now, what do these things means?

1. Task achievement: this is how well you fulfil your job, how well you describe something; how much information you have included; how you have selected information that you put in your writing, and write at least 150 words.

2. Coherence and cohesion: this is how well you chose your paragraphs; how well you organize your information, and how well it flows from beginning to end.

3. Lexical resource: this means vocabulary. This is how much vocabulary you use, and how varied, accurate and appropriate you are with your vocabulary. Spelling errors will hurt your score, misusing word forms will hurt your score. If you say *"~~sales increasing~~"*, it's wrong. Instead, you must say *"sales increased"*

4. Grammatical range and accuracy: obviously this means *"are you making grammar mistakes?"*, and *"are you using complex sentence structures?"* if you're just doing the same structure over and over, *"sales increased"*, then *"sales fluctuated"* and then *"sales plummeted"*. Ok, your grammar is accurate, but all you're giving me is just *past tense, past tense, and past tense.* So you will get a good score for being accurate, but you will get a low score for using the same structure over and over.

What you should be doing in task 1 is you should practice regularly. 7.0 – 8.0 for task 1 writing is very achievable because the language you use for task 1 writing is **very narrow**, and **very limited**. You don't need to use a huge range of language.

IELTS is a game after all. It is a test does exactly a game. It is a system for gaining points and losing points, and there are some rules to test. Therefore, we need to be sure we understand the rules so that we can avoid the penalty.

In order for us to describe diagrams, I would say grammar helps. Yes, of course it does. I need you to pay attention to grammar, sentence structures.

You could get an incredibly high score just by knowing these following structures.

EFFECTIVE SENTENCE STRUCTURES TO GET AN 8.0+

1. Position statement:

- The price of gas _stood at_ $2.75 per gallon.
- In 2005, the sugar export _accounted for_ about 10% of total exports.

2. Movement statements

- There was _a decrease_ in the price of gas/ gas prices.
- There was _an increase_ in the sugar export/ export of sugar/ exported sugar.
- Gas prices/ the price of gas _decreased_.
- The export of sugar/ the sugar export/ the exported sugar _increased_.
- Gas prices/ the price of gas _experienced a decrease_.
- The export of sugar/ the sugar export/ the exported sugar _witnessed an increase_.

3. Time phrases

- From 1990 to 1995
- Between 1990 and 1995
- During/throughout the period from 1995 to 2005
- During a period of 10 years
- Over the (three-month) period (between April and June)
- In 1990
- By 1995
- For 5 years

4. Grammar variations

Connecting sentences together makes your writing more interesting and can help to improve your band score - but you should aim to vary the way you link sentences. Here are a couple options to try instead of just using **"then"**:

- CD sales increased steadily from 2005 until 2010, then fell slightly in the following year.
- CD sales increased steadily from 2005 until 2010, before falling slightly in the following year.
- After increasing steadily from 2005 until 2010, CD sales fell slightly in the following year.

5. Vocabulary variations

Again, these variations increase the range of language you use, which can make your writing more interesting and benefit your band score.

- There was a slight fall in CD sales in 2010.
- (The year) 2010 saw a slight fall in CD sales.
- CD sales experienced a slight fall in 2010.

6. Giving evidence (data)

When you describe the key information in a diagram, it's extremely important to include evidence to support your idea. This means you add data: specific numbers, percentages, etc.

For example:

- CD sales increased slightly from 52 (million) to 70 million units between 2009 and 2010.
- CD sales increased slightly from 52 million units in 2010 to 70 million the following year.
- CD sales increased by eight million units from 2009 to 2010.
- During the period from 1990 to 1995, there was a decrease in gas prices from $2.70 to $2.75 per gallon.
- There was an increase in the sugar export between May and August from about 10% to over 20%.
- Between 1990 and 1995, the price of gas decreased from $2.75 to $2.70 per gallon.
- The sugar export increased from approximately 10% to more than 20% between May and August.

- From 1990 to 1995, the price of gas experienced a decrease from $2.75 to $2.70 per gallon.
- The sugar export witnessed an increase between May and August from around 10% to over 20%.

Vocabulary note

Note the way we use prepositions with numbers and dates:

1998	2000
45%	20%

- In 2000 the number fell **to** 20%.
- In 2000 the number fell **by** 25%.
- The number fell/dropped **from** 45% in 1998 **to** 20% in 2010.
- The number fell/dropped **from** 45% **to** 20% between 1995 and 1997.

You can use a combination of verb + adverb, or adjective + noun, to avoid repeating the same phrases and to add extra meaning:

- There was a significant increase/rise in the number of X.
- The number of X increased/rose significantly.

Notice that you need a preposition when you use the noun form:

- There was an increase in house prices;
- There was a drop of 10% in the number of male students who studied abroad.

Those above are all about the unique things when it comes to your task 1 description. This is a suitable range. So, when it comes to the sentence structures, pay attention to these, and pay attention to the parts of these structures because that is what you will be doing when it comes to describing. Understand that the **grammar** *never changes*, the **verbs** *never change*. They stay the same. You are dealing with a limited number of words, a limited number of structures. *The only thing that changes* is **what you are talking about**. We might be talking about *the purchase of Honda*, or we might talk about *the number of members at a club* or we might talk about *the dollars earned* or *the kilometers travelled* or *the number of books sold*. It doesn't matter. That is the only thing that changes. It is very mathematical

When it comes to task 1, you need to use certain kinds of language:

1. COMPARISON AND SUPERLATIVE LANGUAGE: The language we should use in task 1 writing is the language of **comparison** and **superlative**.

We can compare X and Y by using superlatives.

<u>For example:</u> *Honda was the most popular motorbike.* (Superlative language)

Or: *Honda produced the most sold motorbikes.*

- *Honda was more popular than any other motorbike.* (Comparison language)

- *More males than females chose Honda.*

- *Fewer females than males chose Honda.*

- *Honda was more popular among males than females.*

- *Honda was less popular among females than males.*

- *The most popular means of transport was Honda.*

- *Honda was more popular than any other means of transport.*

- *Honda was the most popular means of transport.*

- *Honda was chosen by more males than females.*

- *A higher percentage of males chose Honda than males.*

- *Compared to/with the number of females, the number of males were considerably higher.*

- *The number of males were considerably higher compared to/with the number of females.*

2. TREND LANGUAGE:

If we have 2 time points (that could be days/weeks/months/years/decades), we need to use trend language. We need to talk about *"increase"*, *"decrease"*.

We could talk about 1990 and 2000, or we could talk about January and June, or we could talk about Monday and Friday. It doesn't matter.

Note: if they give you a diagram with just one year, all we can do is just to compare, we **cannot** use trend language *"increase"*, *"decrease"*, *"fluctuated"*. In other words, we **cannot** talk about movement.

On the other hand, if they give you two years, three years, or four years, they still want comparison, but now they also want **trend language**. They also want you to talk about movement. These are really two basic groups of language that you need to use to describe diagrams: **comparison** and **trend language**.

Let's build some vocabulary. Here is a list of verbs, adverbs, adjectives and nouns that you need to use in task 1 writing.

LANGUAGE OF TRENDS: SENTENCE STRUCTURE AND VOCABULARY

Meaning	Verb	Noun	Adjectives	Adverbs
Go down	• decline • decrease • drop • fall • go down • plummet • plunge	• decline • decrease • drop • fall • go down • plummet • plunge	• sharp • rapid • quick • considerable • significant • substantial • steady • gradual • moderate • slight • slow	• sharply • rapidly • quickly • considerably • significantly • substantially • steadily • gradually • moderately • slightly • slowly
Go up	• climb • go up • grow • increase • jump • rise • rocket	• climb • go up • growth • increase • rise		

No change ───	• Level off at • remain the same • remain unchanged • remain constant • remain stable • stay constant • stay stable • stay steady • keep unchanged	• A levelling off at		
Constant change /\/\	• fluctuate • vary (around)	• fluctuation • variation		

Change of direction				
	• To bottom out at • To hit a low point/the lowest/the largest of	• A low of • A high of		
	• To peak at • To reach a peak of			

	To stand at To start/begin at To end/finish at			

Grammatical structures used to describe trends.	Time phrases
There + Be + Adj + Noun + In + Noun Phrase • There was <u>a significant increase</u> in the number of unemployed people during the period. • There was <u>a slight increase</u> in the gold price/ the price of gold between 2005 and 2010.	• From 1995 to 2005 • For 10 years • Between 1995 and 2005 • During/throughout the period from 1995 to 2005 • During a period of 10 years • Over the (three-month) period (between April and June)
Noun Phrase + Verb + Adverb • The number of unemployed people increased significantly during the period. • The gold price/ the price of gold increased slightly.	

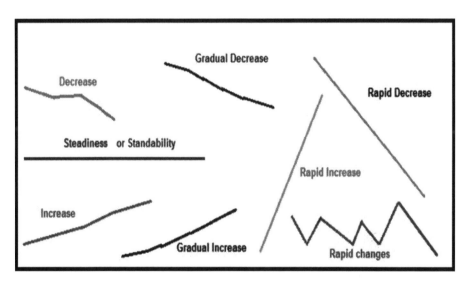

Examples:

The overall sale of the company slightly increased by 10% in 2005.

A downward trend *The consumption for Hamburger witnessed a downward trend over the period.*	
To fall steadily *Expenditure on landline phones fell steadily over the 10-year period.*	
To drop/decrease slightly *The proportion of bus commuters dropped/decreased slightly to 15% in 2002.*	
To rise gradually *The proportions of elderly people in the UK rose gradually over the next 20 years.*	

To level off *The unemployment rate <u>levelled off</u> at 18% in 2008.*	
To drop suddenly *The figure <u>dropped suddenly</u> to 10% in 1975.*	
To increase/climb sharply *The number of people using computers <u>increased/climbed</u> sharply from 2002 to 2005.*	
An upward trend *There was <u>an upward trend</u> in the number of people using the Internet between 1995 and 2005.*	

Note that **"plunge"** and **"plummet"** <u>do not</u> **take adverbs** because what they mean is a big decrease.

We can say *"decreased considerably / sharply / dramatically / significantly / substantially"* or "plunged", or "plummeted".

But, we **must not** say,

"plummeted ~~considerably / sharply / dramatically / significantly / substantially~~" or

"plunged ~~considerably / sharply / dramatically / significantly / substantially~~"

No need to use those two verbs *"plunge"* and *"plummet"* with an adverb.

Decreased sharply equals *plummeted*. They mean the same thing.

Likewise, **"rocket"** <u>does not</u> **take adverbs.** So to say *increased significantly, rose sharply*, they mean the same thing as *rocketed*. <u>A big/sharp increase,</u> so **no adverbs** for rocketed.

There are some things I need you to be aware of here. I want you to know that **steadily** and **gradually** mean the same thing. *Slightly* is something means <u>different</u>. **Steadily** and **gradually** *mean over a period of time*. *Slightly* means <u>how much deals with amount</u>. **Steadily** and **gradually** mean <u>a gradual change</u> like a child growth; he or she grows gradually/ he or she grows over time.

Levelled off **& stabilized**

These are <u>flat changes</u> or <u>no changes</u> really, but I want you to be aware that *levelled off* and *stabilized* *always happen <u>after another trend</u>*. You can say, for example, *"the figure <u>remained the same</u> before increasing/ the figure <u>remained stable</u> before increasing/ the figure <u>remained unchanged</u> before increasing/ the figure <u>remained constant</u> before increasing"*. However, we **cannot** use "stabilized or levelled off" in this case. Stabilized and levelled off always happen after another trend. For example, *sales fluctuated before they levelled off/ sales fluctuated before they stabilized*. **Don't ever** use stabilized and levelled off <u>to start your description</u>.

Fluctuation

You can say *fluctuated significantly/ fluctuated wildly* (big changes) or *fluctuated slightly* (small changes).

The birthday <u>fluctuated significantly/wildly</u> between 2000 and 2005.

Reached a low

"Reach" always happen after a movement. "A high" is always <u>behind a point of the diagram</u>. We **shouldn't say** ~~reached a high~~, instead we say *started at a high/ began at a high*.

We can say *reached a low/ started at a low/ began at a low*

Car sales <u>reached a low of</u> 15.000 in 2000.

Reached a peak

"A peak" is always up and down. A peak can be <u>a high</u> but it doesn't have to be. For example, *reached two peaks before reaching a high.*

The number of people who were unemployed <u>reached a peak of</u> 2000 people in 2015.

The number of tourists <u>reached a peak of</u> 15 million in 1995.

Stood at

You can use "stood at" <u>at anywhere on the graph</u> you want *(<u>at the beginning</u> it stood at, <u>afterward</u> it stood at, <u>then</u> it stood at", <u>then</u> it stood at, <u>then</u> it stood at something else).* "Stood at" works for anything on the graph.

The number of sales <u>stood at</u> 4 million in 2010.

The number of people travelling to London <u>stood at</u> 26 million in 2005.

Started at/ began at

You can use "started at/ began at" at the beginning.

In 2000, the figure for Internet users <u>started at</u> approximately 50 million.

The amount of meat consumed weekly <u>began at</u> about 150 grams.

Ended at/ finished at

You can use "ended at/ finished at" at the end.

The figure <u>finished at</u> over 50%.

Dipped/decreased slightly

Expenditure on furniture <u>dipped slightly</u> from 9% to 7% between 2002 and 2005.

Coffee sales <u>decreased slightly</u> between June and August.

Examples:

Coffee sales began at 50 thousand dollars, then decreased slightly to 48 thousand dollars. Subsequently, sales plunged and reached a low of 40 thousand dollars between June and

August. Afterwards, coffee sales rocketed to a high of 70 thousand dollars. Sales remained stable before decreasing and stabilizing at…

Started at a high…then it fell slightly/ declined slightly/ dropped slightly/ fell steadily/ declined gradually…then it levelled off/ stabilized/ remained unchanged/ remained stable/ remained the same/ maintained the same figure.

Sales soared/ rocketed/ rose dramatically/ grew sharply/ increased substantially.

"Soared" really is the same as "rocketed".

Increased slightly/increased gradually.

The number of people using the Internet increased slightly between 1995 and 2005.

From 2002 to 2004, CD sales in the UK increased gradually from 3 to 4 million - a rise of 30%.

Experienced/witnessed/saw a decrease/a decline/a rise/an increase

Laptop prices experienced a decrease/ a decline.

Laptop prices underwent a decrease/ a decline.

The price of laptop saw a fall/ decrease/ a decline.

The price of laptop witnessed a fall/ decrease/ a decline.

As far as I know, this method allows you to *have a variety while maintaining accuracy and limiting what you need to learn*. I don't need you to learn everything. I just need to learn these things. These are simple structures, because there are no time, and no figure. There are no adjectives or adverbs here. These are very simple. Let's look at these again:

The purchase of Honda increased slightly from…..to….

Honda sales grew slightly from nearly…to…..

Honda sales decreased substantially, falling from…to…

Sales of Yamaha rocketed.

Sales of Yamaha soared.

Sales of Yamaha increased substantially.

You **don't need to get creative**, this is not poetry. This is a boring technical writing. You need to **recognize the verbs**, and then you need to **recognize the nouns, adverbs and adjectives.** Just use what I gave you, learn the simple words here, learn the simple grammar and you will find that you have an incredible range of words and structures just by using the combination of the basics I've mentioned above.

Other basic language:

A doubling means twice (10% ➔ 20%)

A tripling means three times (10% ➔ 30%)

Rocketed = soared = increased substantially/ significantly/ dramatically = plunged = plummeted

Decrease = decline = fall = experience a decrease

So all that you need to know is just some basic things, and you are able to change the words around a little bit and **that's the key**. You **don't need** to learn a ton of grammar. You just need to learn this grammar and how to use these words. That's it, and then you will become a master of IELTS task 1 writing. Now, I would like to warn you that **the biggest problem** my students have when it comes to task 1 writing is that **they don't believe it's simple**.

When it comes to give you <u>dates and times</u>, and to give you <u>figures</u>, you <u>don't need to use prepositions</u>. What prepositions do we need? *From, in, to* or maybe *at.* So, even the prepositions that you need are very limited, you just need to pay attention and notice what is going to be used in the same structure over and over again. The only thing that will change will be basic things here are:

- What happens or happened?
- The figure?
- What's being measures? (The unit of measurement)
- The dates? (Time)

It's totally mathematical. It's a formula. Got it?

Now, **how do we put these things together to make a report?**

Here is the method.

I don't want you to be nervous or confused in the exam, I want you to be more confident like *"all right, the first thing is this...next thing is that...and the next thing is this…...and the next thing is you know how to write a report excellently"*.

TASK 1 WRITING PROCESS TO MAXIMIZE SCORE

1. Read Summary: What they will be giving you in task 1 writing is they will give you a diagram with a description. This description is called a summary. The summary is used to tell you what you are looking at, and it will tell you exactly that, so you must read the summary carefully before writing.

Example: *"The table below shows how many tourists from five countries visiting Australia in different years from 1991 and 1999."*

When you look at the diagram, the first step should be asking yourself

- What's the verb tense? Or what are the verb tenses? (Past tense)
- Look at the summary, look at the diagram and ask yourself
  - What is measured? (the number of tourists)
  - Unit of Measurement? (thousand)

  We need to be accurate about <u>what is being measured</u> and <u>the unit of measurement</u>.

2. Analyze Trends:

- Look at the general trend. It's quite easy. You simply look <u>from the beginning to the end</u>. You don't need to worry about the middle. You only should look at the beginning and the end *(did it increase?, did it remain the same?, or did it decrease?)*
- After looking at the general trend, you should look at a couple of the other things. First of all you see if <u>any peaks</u>, <u>any dips</u>, <u>any fluctuations</u>, <u>anything is going in the middle between the beginning and the end</u>.
- Superlatives (highest, least, most, fewest). For example, *which country accounted for the most or and which country accounted for the fewest visitors?*

3. What are the main points? The main points are <u>the most important features</u> *(<u>the most important trends</u>, <u>some general comparisons</u> and <u>some general</u>*

superlatives).

I should have an idea about what the whole diagram looks like – they're on your main points, and when it comes to the main points, I would say *"overall, the number of visitors from all five countries <u>increased</u>, meanwhile the US and the UK <u>accounted for the most tourists</u> throughout the period"* 2 sentences. Now, what I just gave you is going to give you a 7.0+ on the task achievement. You need to give me **general trends** and **some superlatives**. You need to have a general idea of trends and comparisons in your main points.

4. The next thing you should be doing here is you need to **organize your paragraphs**

I'll tell you to do 3 paragraphs here: your **introduction**, your **overview**, and **2 body paragraphs**.

Your introduction should be a paraphrased summary.

Your overview should be the main points that have <u>trends</u> and some <u>comparisons</u>.

You can use <u>some expressions for your overview</u> as below:

- *The graph shows (information about) / indicates / illustrates / highlight (the data about)…*
- *As the graph shows*
- *It is clear from the graph (that)*
- *As is shown by the graph*
- *It can be seen from the graph (that)*
- *As can be clearly seen from the graph,*
- *From the graph, it is clear (that)*
- *As is illustrated by the graph,*

You will get marks on your main points. If you don't include any main points in your overview paragraph even though your grammar and vocabulary are perfect, you are not going to get higher than a 5.0 in task achievement because there is no clear overview. If you want to get a 7.0+ in task achievement, you need to <u>add the main points</u> that <u>have trends and some comparisons</u>.

Your body paragraphs need to be organized logically. For example, if we have 5 countries to look at. We may organize the body paragraphs by their figures (3 countries have the highest figures, we will describe them in one paragraph, and with the smallest figures, we will describe them in the other paragraph)

STRUCTURE: Paraphrase Summary...Main Point...Describe

Once you figure out the verb tense, what is measured? Unit of measurement. Once you analyzed and looked at the general trends, and you figured out the main points. Now you can describe these things in 15 minutes. It will be good.

So, the tough part in IETLS writing task 1 will be practicing, looking at enough diagrams that you can look at things quickly and go to take notes and figure out what's happening, and practicing the grammar and vocabulary enough, you will become automatic. If you do that, task 1 will be easier for you to deal with your IELTS test. I promise. Because it's a boring stuff, there is no creativity at all. It's just looking at what they are giving you, making a few corrections, a few grammar changes. And the grammar changes you are making is that you just change verbs, nouns, adjectives and adverbs. These are simple stuff.

TASK 1 MARKING AND ASSESSMENT

- Organize, present, and compare data...do you describe the most important points?
- Use English grammar and vocabulary
- Use appropriate style and content
- Write in a way that the reader can follow

ADVICE

- Of course, grammar helps, but you should also focus on using various sentence structures! Don't use the same sentence structures over and over.
- Read as much as possible, you will understand how to be a more effective writer by observing other writers.
- Write as much as you can.
- You have to choose your information carefully (which figures do you want to get without talking about every little change?)
- Practicing going from verbs, adverbs to nouns, adjectives as well as practice changing your noun forms. For example, I want to talk about the production of films, and coffee from Viet Nam. We want to get rid of the preposition so that the noun will become the adjective. So we have the production of films will become film production (film in this case is an adjective so it is a singular form), and likewise, coffee from Viet Nam will become Vietnamese coffee; or fell gradually will become there was a gradual fall. You need to switch between nouns and adjectives, verbs and adverbs, and you need to say "the development of the new products" will become "new product development", "number of theme park visitors" will become "theme park visitor numbers"; "sugar import" will become "imported sugar"; "quality of food in super market" will become "super market food quality"; "investment in research" will become "research investment"; "the level of unemployment" will become "the unemployment level"
- One more thing is that you need to do some simple comparison words. You'll need to be able to have flexibility to use comparison structures.

Note: Even a graph that shows you something going from the past, through the present, in the future, I would still say that you **don't** need to use present perfect in your writing. I would say you'd better just need to focus on using past tense and future tense. If you want to get a higher vocabulary and grammar score when you are dealing with the future tense, you can start talking about future perfect. It's a lot easier to use and a lot more natural sounding.

Don't talk about many trends, just two trends for three points.

USEFUL TIME EXPRESSIONS

- (In) the period from…..to……/ between……and *((in) the period from January to April... between January and April...)*
- During *(during the first two years...)*
- In the first/ last three months of the year
- Over the period from…….to……..
- Over the next...for the following... *(for the following five years... Over the next five years...)*
- Over a ten-year period
- After that/ then
- Until
- Throughout the year/ throughout the period/ each month of the year
- Subsequently
- For the rest of the year
- In January/ it began the year/ at the beginning of the year/ at the beginning of the period
- In December/ the end of the year

You should pay attention to how you are using them. Keep your sentences short but clear by using those kinds of phrases. **Notice** that your sentences should be relatively short. You don't need to write long sentences to impress people. Long sentences tend to get grammar problems. What easier to read is a three line sentence or two line sentence. What is easier to remember, a 100 page book or 10 page book? Of course, a 10 page book. So, keep things short and use the proper linking phrases to allow your overall sentences to connect. **That's the key**.

LANGUAGE OF ESTIMATION

- Just over
- Nearly
- About
- Around
- Almost
- Approximately
- Just about
- Very nearly
- Just over
- More than
- Less than

As the graph shows, in January, the figure _stood at_ more than 1500.

Regarding novel sales, in January, the figure _stood at_ just over 1500 _before declining steadily_ to a low of nearly 90,000.

USEFUL WORDS FOR PARAPHRASING A SUMMARY

Original sentence: _The chart below shows…_

Paraphrased sentence: _the line graph/ the line chart indicates/depicts/reveals/illustrates…_

- _Sales = income = revenue = turnover = how much money was made._

- _The income rate = the income level = the level of income = the rate of income = the level of revenue = the revenue rate = the revenue level_

- _New York City bookstore = bookstore in New York City_

- _Proportion = percentage = rate_

- _The proportion of = the percentage of = the figure for._

- _From 2000 to 2005 = between 2000 and 2005 = Over a period of (5) years._

- _The elderly = elderly people = senior citizens._

- _Spending = expenditure._

- _Information = data_

- _Levels of unemployment = Unemployment rate._

- _Poverty rate = Level of poverty._

- _Production = manufacture = be produced = be made = be manufactured_

Note:

The examiner **doesn't care** about what you say, they care about <u>how well you use English</u>

The figure for X

What is **X**? Whatever you are talking about.

<u>For example:</u> *the figure for novel sales, the figure for action films, the figure for whatever it said on the diagram.* This works all the time. If you find in the exam that you have 10 minutes, you don't have time to be killed with your vocabulary. "The figure for" <u>works</u>.

Or you can use "X's figure". For example, *romance film's figure*

The contribution of X

"Contribution" means <u>how much do you give to something</u>, <u>how much do you give to the whole/ the total</u>. **"Contribution"** works when we <u>talk about percentages</u> because "percentage" is looking at the whole (100%). So, here I can say:

The contribution of romance films stood at more than 50% in 1990.

Romance film's contribution stood at more than 50% in 1990.

Romance film contributed more than 50% in 1990.

What another word for "film types"?

Film kinds = film types = film genres

A genre is a type of something. For example, <u>action/horror</u> is a genre of film, <u>romance</u> is a genre of film, etc.

<u>Examples:</u> *three kinds of films = three genres of films = three types of films* (NOT ~~three film types~~ or ~~three film kinds~~)

TASK 1 WRITING RULES

1. You must write **150 words minimum, 220 words maximum**. If you write more than 220 words, you will face a penalty. You won't have enough time to complete your task 2 writing.

2. **You must skip lines between paragraphs.** This allows you to do a couple of important things here. Skipping lines is going to make your writing neater. That is important. Remember that the writing test, we are dealing with the human being. Who is the human being? The examiner, and we need to make this guy happy. Right away, I want the examiner when they have a pile of writings in front of them, and they might not feel well, they might be hungry, they might have had an argument with their boyfriend or girlfriend; they might just be sick of a pile of writings. When they turn to look at your writing, and I want the first thing they think about when they see your writing is that you are *a neat organized student*. I want you to give them the first positive impression. They often have to choose between a 5.5 or 6.0; 6.5 or 7.0; I want them to have all reasons to give you a 7.0, not 5.5 or 6.0, so you should make your examiner happy and be neat.

3. **Keep it simple:** you should use exactly the list of task 1 vocabulary, sentence structures that I have given you in this book. **Do not get creativity.** Trust me, you are probably wrong if you are creative. My experience of over four years of teaching IELTS for many different levels of students. They do not do well with creativity when it comes to IELTS writing task 1. Please do what I tell you to do. It's simple, but it will give you a high score.

4. **Corrections:** it's great that some of you do your writing, and then you look at it, you think about it and you fix things/mistakes in your writing. That's awesome! If you catch your mistakes before your teacher catch them, you are doing a learning. Who need to do a learning? You or your teacher? **You.** I very highly encourage you to write these kinds of reports using your knowledge, taking your time, being careful and then walking away from the reports. Go and take a nap, watch TV, have some coffee, whatever, just forget about your homework, and then come back with your fresh eyes and fresh mind, then read your writing

out loud. I promise to you that your ears will catch grammar mistakes because you hear a lot more English than you ever read. Don't you? Yes, same thing with the native speakers.

MOST COMMON MISTAKES STUDENTS MAKE IN TASK 1 WRITING

1. Adverb vs adjective

A slight increase/decrease. (NOT a ~~slightly~~ increase/decrease).

2. Copy the summary

This just means you do not paraphrase the summary enough. That's a big problem. Be sure you paraphrase the summary as much as you can.

3. Misusing words or phrases.

You might say: Sales ~~levelled off~~ and then decreased (it's wrong, because we always use "levelled off" after another trend.)

So, *levelled off* is misused in this case.

Or, you might say: sales ~~reduced~~. (We don't use "reduced" this way)

Instead we say *sales decreased/declined*

4. Question mark

No question mark in task 1 writing. This means either a confusing word, a phrase, may be a sentence or may be a whole paragraph. The examiner will not know what you are talking about. The grammar is so stuffed that they cannot understand what you are trying to say, and they cannot easily fix your grammar.

So what are you going to do with this kind of sentence?

First, don't try to fix the mistakes that you have. Don't look at back your grammar over and over again. Instead, look at what you are saying and ask yourself what you were trying to say. You wrote it, so you know what you are trying to describe, then look at back the task 1 language, words, and phrases I gave you above, and start writing that sentence, or whole paragraph over. Don't try to fix what you have, take what you have and throw away and put something new in there.

5. Wrong verb tense use.

Pay your attention to the verb tense.

6. Don't use figures in your introduction and overview (no need to give numbers in your main point)

7. Capital letters and lowercase letter.

8. Redundant or needlessly repeat word phrases or information. It creates extra words but it doesn't give new information. Therefore, you don't need to keep saying a word or a phrase over and over again. Instead, you can use "it", "this", "this figure" to replace that word or phrase.

9. Collocation issues

You don't put words together properly.

10. Your main point lacks either comparison or trend language, and you cannot get a 7.0+ in task achievement without it.

TIPS:

Go home and rewrite the task 1 reports that they are already fixed by your teacher. Just take 15 -20 minutes to rewrite it. Try to change every sentence structure that you wrote in your report with a new structure. Practice using different structures because in the exam that will help you a lot. You will have a variety, you will have accuracy and make your report well organized. And of course you will get a high score.

FUTURE TENSE (LANGUAGE OF ESTIMATION)

STRUCTURE 1:

The prediction/expectation/projection/forecast/anticipations/likelihood + *shows/reveals/indicates/*is that there will be a dramatic increase in the number of car users.

The anticipation shows/reveals/indicates/is that there will be an increase in the price of food from 20 dollars in 2005 to 25 dollars in 2025.

The forecast shows/reveals/indicates/is that the price of food will undergo/witness/experience an increase from 20 dollars in 2005 to 25 dollars in 2025.

STRUCTURE 2:

It is predicted/expected/projected/estimated/ anticipated/forecast/likely that the number of car users will increase dramatically.

It is predicted/expected/anticipated/forecast/estimated that the price of food will increase from 20 dollars in 2005 to 25 dollars in 2025.

It is predicted/expected/anticipated/forecast/estimated that the price of food will undergo/witness/experience an increase from 20 dollars in 2005 to 25 dollars in 2025.

STRUCTURE 3:

The number of car users are predicted/expected/projected/estimated/ anticipated/forecast to increase dramatically.

The price of food is predicted/expected/anticipated/forecast/estimated to decline from 20 dollars in 2000 to 10 dollars in 2025.

The price of food is predicted/expected/anticipated/forecast/estimated to experience a decline from 20 dollars in 2000 to 10 dollars in 2025.

FUTURE PERFECT: WILL + HAVE + PAST PARTICIPLE

Let's talk about future perfect. I will not talk about future continuous, I will only talk about future perfect because usually my students find it hard to give me a range of structures as well as another verb form.

What is future perfect?

Future perfect is a verb form that we use to indicate <u>a completed action at some time</u> in the future.

So if I say *"tonight I will eat dinner"*. This means some time in the evening, I'll be eating. It's not clear.

But if I say *"<u>by 9 o'clock</u> I <u>will have eaten</u> dinner"*. That means at night o'clock, I <u>have finished</u> my dinner. I'm done. The action is completed.

Note: with future perfect, we <u>always need a time</u>.

Instead of saying *"the price of food is expected to decline to 20 dollars in 2020"*

We can say *"the price of food is expected to <u>have declined</u> to 20 dollars by 2020"*

Or *"the price of food is expected to <u>have experienced</u> a decline to 20 dollars by 2020"*

Or *"it is expected that the price of food <u>will have declined</u> to 20 dollars by 2020"*

Try to give <u>a variety of structures</u>, <u>be accurate</u>, <u>use a variety of verbs</u>, <u>use the future perfect</u>, you will get a higher score.

Understand that we can use a combination of past and future tenses.

In 2010, the figure stood at... (Past tense)..., but it's expected to increase slightly to... (Future tense).

"Respectively" & "in turn"

Jack and Jill are tall and fat <u>respectively</u>.

Who is tall?

Answer: Jack

Who is fat?

Answer: Jill

My first and second pair of shoes are red and white <u>respectively</u>.

What is the color of <u>the second pair of shoes</u>?

Answer: white

What is the color of <u>the first pair of shoes</u>?

Answer: red

So, we always use "respectively" and "in turn" to talk about two things that we talk about in a sentence.

CORRELATION

We use "as" and "while" to show two things happening at the same time.

As I watched TV, I ate dinner.

While I drove my motorbike, I listened to music.

While I swam in the ocean, my family sat on the beach.

MAJORITY

What is the majority?

"The majority" means more than 50%.

How about 51% & 49%?

The difference between 51% & 49% is <u>so slight</u>.

51%: *a small majority of* (NOT ~~huge~~ majority).

>75%: *a vast majority of*

We use the definite article "the" + majority when we have only one majority.

49%: *a minority/ just under half*

11%: *a small/ tiny minority of*

We use the indefinite article "a" + minority when we don't have the only one minority. Besides 49%, we also have 40%, 25%, etc.

Examples:

32% of all tourists = nearly a third of all tourists.

47% of cars = just under half of cars.

63% of all funding = nearly two-thirds of all funding.

TASK 1 WRITING SAMPLES

LINE CHART

The graph below shows the differences in wheat exports over three different areas. Write a report for a university lecturer describing the information shown below. Write at least 150 words.

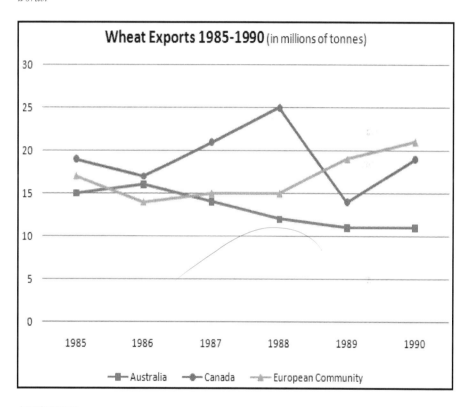

Wheat Exports 1985-1990 (in millions of tonnes)

ANSWER:

The line graph compares three regions in terms of exports of wheat between 1985 and 1990.

Overall, the three regions experienced different trends in the time period. While the wheat export in Canada and European countries rose with some fluctuations, the export in Australia fell over time.

As the graph shows, Australia's wheat export figure started at 15 million tons in 1985 followed by a small increase to around 16 million tons in 1986. Then, it declined steadily until it fell to just over 10 million tons in 1990. Regarding Canada's exports, in 1985 they shipped approximately 19 million tons of wheat. This figure fell to about 17 million in 1986, but then their exports experienced considerable growth to 25 million tons in 1988. Afterward, the figure plunged to below 15 million in 1989, but then subsequently rose to just under 20 million in 1990.

By contrast, the wheat exports from the European Community experienced an increase in the six year period. In 1985, nearly 16 million tons were exported, but this number fell to about 14 million in 1986. Then, the exports increased to exactly 15 million tons in 1987 and 1988 before witnessing steady growth to 19 million and 21 million tons in 1989 and 1990, respectively.

(209 words)

·

BAR CHART

SAMPLE 1:

The chart below shows the amount of leisure time enjoyed by men and women of different employment status.

Write a report for a university lecturer describing the information shown below.

You should write at least 150 words in 20 minutes for this task.

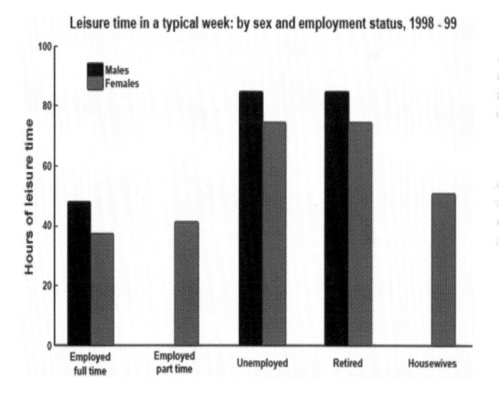

Leisure time in a typical week: by sex and employment status, 1998 - 99

ANSWER:

The bar chart compares the amount of free time per week that males and females of five categories of employment status had between 1998 and 1999.

It is clear that men enjoyed more hours of leisure time per week than women in three out of five categories. However, only figures for women are shown in two categories, namely employed part-time and housewives.

Regarding the full-time employed, obviously men had slightly more leisure time than women, with approximately 45 hours of free time per week, compared to around 38 hours for women. Obviously, unemployed and retired people of both genders enjoyed the most hours of leisure time. Moreover, the figures for retired males and females were exactly the same as those for the unemployed, at around 85 and 78 hours of free time per week, respectively.

Housewives enjoyed 50 hours of spare time, a little more than part-time working women who had just over 40 leisure hours each week. No data is given for men in either of these categories.

169 words.

You should spend about 20 minutes on this task.

The following bar chart shows the different modes of transport used to travel to and from work in one European city in 1960, 1980 and 2000.

Summarize the information by selecting and reporting the main features and make comparisons where relevant.

Write at least 150 words.

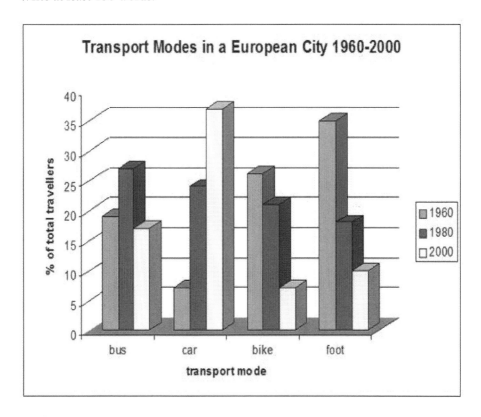

ANSWER:

The bar chart illustrates the information about the proportion of travelers who used different types of vehicles to commute to work in a European city during a period from 1960 to 2000.

Overall, the percentage of commuters who used cars rose steadily over the period, while the proportion of people who travelled by other means of transport fell.

In 1960, approximately 35% of people commuted to work on foot, compared to only about 5% of people travelled by car. The percentage of those who used bikes and buses were around 25% and 18% respectively. However, in 1980 travelling by bus was by far the most popular transport mode, accounting for over 25% of total travelers, whereas only 17% of people travelling on foot. The figures for bike and car were around 20% and 22% respectively.

At the end of the period, more than 35% of commuters used cars to commute to work in this city in 2000, which was much higher than the figure for bus users, at around 16%. The percentage of those who travelled to work on foot and by bike fell to 9% and 6% respectively.

189 words

TABLE

The table below gives information about the average annual spending of university students in three different countries.

Countries	Country A	Country B	Country C
Total spending	US$ 5000	4500	1500
Different living costs			
Accommodation	45%	35%	30%
Food	22%	28%	36%
Books	3%	9%	21%
Leisure	22%	23%	12%
Others	8%	5%	1%

The given table compares the percentage of expenditure which college students from 3 countries spend on different living expenses each year.

Overall, the total spending of students in country A was higher than the expenditure of students in countries B and C. In all the countries, students spent the highest proportion of their budget on accommodation and food.

In country A, the total spending of students is highest, at 5000$ per year, compared with $4500 and $1500 for students in countries B and C respectively.

Accommodation accounts for 45% of the total expenditure of students in country A, while the proportions were lower for students in country B at 35%, and country C, at only 30%. However, in term of food, students in country C spend the largest percentage of their money on it, accounting for 36%. The figures for country A and B are only 22% and 28% respectively.

Students in country C also spent a high percentage of their budget on books, at 21%, compared with 9% for students in country B and just 3% for students in country A. By contrast, students in countries A and B spent 22% and 23% respectively of their budget on leisure, while students in country C spent only 12% of their total money on this category.

196 words.

PIE CHART

The pie charts below show the average household expenditures in Japan and Malaysia in the year 2010.

Summarise the information by selecting and reporting the main features, and make comparisons where relevant.

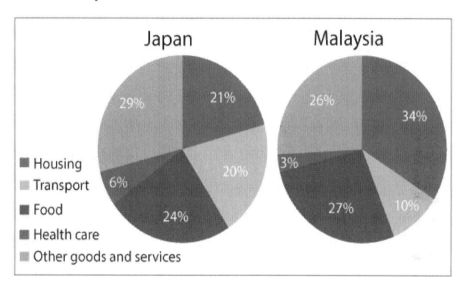

ANSWER

The pie charts compare the average household spending in Japan and Malaysia in terms of five important categories in 2010.

Overall, it is clear that Japanese and Malaysian people spent the largest proportion of their budget on just three categories, namely housing, food and other goods and services. Moreover, the expenditures on healthcare and transport in Japan were double the figures for Malaysia.

In Malaysian households, the greatest proportion of spending was on housing, which represented 34% of the total expenditure, while in Japan, the figure for this category was just 21%. Japanese householders spent the largest amount of their income on other goods and services, at 29%. Meanwhile, the rate of spending on this category in Malaysia was slightly lower, at 26%. In terms of food, the percentages of expenses for both nations were relatively similar, at 27% for Malaysia and 24% for Japan.

In both countries, the smallest proportion of spending was on health care. In Malaysia, this accounted for 3% of the total household expenses, while the figure for transport represented 10%. These figures were exactly doubled in Japan which were 6% and 20% respectively.

188 words.

MAP

MAPS are becoming a lot more common. The language that we use to describe graphs like bar charts, tables, line graphs, would not be used to describe maps. We should need to use new language to describe maps.

MAP LANGUAGE

LANGUAGE OF DIRECTION:

In the north: within an area. *(California is in the west of the United States/ Phu My Hung is in the south of HCM city.)*

To the north: to be used for comparison/ outside an area *(China is to the north of Vietnam/ Cambodia is to the west of Vietnam.)*

In the southwest: *Florida is in the southeast of the United States.*

To the southwest: *The entrance was moved to the southwest of the building.*

LANGUAGE OF LOCATION:

Be located/situated in: *The shopping mall was located/ situated in the center of the city was knocked down to make way for a new university.*

Opposite: *A restaurant has been built on the opposite side of the road where the shop used to be.*

Next to: *A new car park has been constructed next to the hotel.*

Along: *there was a new sidewalk along the river.*

Across from: *The park is across from the school.*

GRAMMAR:

The grammar for Map is quite simple that you should use passive voice in paste tense.

VERBS TO DESCRIBE MAP:

Buildings: *Demolished, knocked down, constructed, built, erected*

The apartment was demolished.

The school located in the south of the city was knocked down/ demolished to make way for a car park.

The building <u>was erected</u> on the bank of the river.

Areas:

A new residential area <u>was built</u> in place of the park.

A golf course <u>was constructed</u> to the west of the airport.

The park <u>disappeared</u>.

An airport <u>appeared</u>.

Trees: *cut down/ chopped down, removed, uprooted*

In the north of the river all trees <u>were cut down/ chopped down</u>.

All the trees <u>were removed/ uprooted and replaced by</u> a factory.

Factories/facilities: *established, installed, placed, put in*

An airport <u>was established/ installed</u>.

Don't say: *a house was ~~installed/ established~~.*

Areas and zones:

An urban area = a city

A rural area = a countryside

An industrial area = factory, manufacturing, processing

Residential area = houses

Recreational area & Entertainment area

We use recreational areas to usually talk about things like <u>parks</u> or <u>other green areas</u> that people do activities.

Entertainment area is actually <u>part of a commercial area</u>. When you go to <u>sing karaoke</u>, or when you go and <u>watch a film</u> at the theater, you are in the area that <u>the focus is money</u>.

General main points: *More urban, less rural, more developed, more modern.*

METHOD FOR WRITING MAP

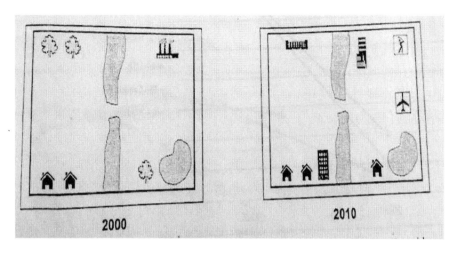

Pick a side of the town. Divide the town into two parts, the north and the south or the east and the west. Find the way to divide the town.

On the west side of the river, *in the north,* trees <u>were cut down/chopped down</u> and <u>replaced</u> by a stadium by 2010. *In the south,* an apartment building/complex <u>was constructed</u> *between* some private homes and the river.

Looking at/To the east, a hotel <u>was built/erected</u> *in the north, along the river. (To the) east of this,* an industrial area/zone <u>was demolished</u> and <u>replaced by / made way for / made way for the development of / transformed into / converted into</u> a golf course. In the *center/central area,* an airport <u>was established</u>. Just *to the west of the lake,* by 2010, a residential area <u>was developed</u> after trees were removed.

"To the north of this / next to the railway station, the residential area <u>was transformed into</u> an industrial area."

Noted: transformed into and converted into: this means to change something.

We **cannot** say *"the apartment was ~~transformed into~~ the factory"*

We **cannot** say *"the trees were ~~transformed into~~ the airport"*, we **cannot** change a tree into an airport. Instead, we can say *"the trees were chopped down and replaced with the airport."*

We **only can use** transformed into and converted into when we are talking about an area.

Ex: *the park was transformed into the airport* (because a park is an area of land)

We can *transform a rural area into an urban area.*

The neighborhood was transformed completely.

The old houses were rebuilt.

Very few trees remained.

Trees were chopped down/ uprooted/ cleared/ cleared away.

The area was removed, but remained vacant/ remained undeveloped.

ARTICLE:

We use "a" for new, and "the" for old

Ex: *in the south, the residential area was replaced by a warehouse (it's new).*

In the north, the residential area was removed to make way for the development of a stadium (it's new).

Don't say "~~the left/right side of town~~". But **it's ok** for you **to say** "on the left/right side of the map"

Apartment building = apartment complex

MAP SAMPLE

The maps show changes that took place in Youngsville in New Zealand over a 25 year period from 1980 to 2005.

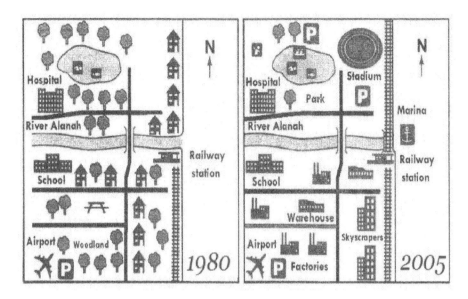

ANSWER:

The maps illustrate the developments which took place in the coastal town of Youngsville between 1980 and 2005.

Overall, a comparison of the two maps reveals a complete transformation from a largely rural to a mainly urban area.

In the year 1980, the town was a much greener residential area with a large number of trees and individual houses, but during the next 25 years, the town saw a number of significant changes. The most noticeable is that all of the trees in the south of the River Alanah were chopped down, with all the houses along the railway line being demolished to make way for skyscrapers. Moreover, a new industrial zone with warehouses and factories sprang up around the school and airport.

In contrast, only a few trees in the north of the river remained. The woodland was cleared and converted into a golf course, a park, and car parting facilities. Further developments were the construction of a stadium next to the north-east corner of the lake and the extension of the railway line from the river running directly to the north. A Marina was also constructed at the mouth of the river.

194 words.

PROCESS

<u>Type 1:</u> **Man-made process:** how things are made, how things are produced, how things are manufactured, how things are done.

<u>Type 2:</u> **Natural process:** it's the most difficult to learn and to teach because there is no clear and exact way to teach you about the language. I could spend a week talking about the natural process and still not feel prepared for the exam.

One of the really nice things about **man-made process** report is the fact that the grammar is very simple, what you need to do with your sentence structure is very simple, however, there is a big challenge with these kinds of report. The big challenge is you don't know anything about how to make a chocolate candy/brick…, and the vocabulary can be a little bit difficult.

Let's learn about easy things about process reports. With process reports we will be asked to analyze and illustrate a diagram and describe a man-made process…how to do something, how to make something. For example, they may show you *how to bring water from the city to the countryside…*

MAN-MADE PROCESS

1. You will be using **passive present tense** (is/are + V3). This is different from what we have with MAPS. Maps we use with passive tense. Remember we use passive tense because we don't want to focus on the actor or the subject of the sentence, we want to focus on the action or verb of the sentence. We don't care that the investors built the house, we only care about how the house was built. Likewise. For man-made process, you may use passive tense, but present tense (is/are, NOT ~~was/were~~) because we don't care about who made the chocolate, we only care about <u>how the chocolate is made</u>. You will be using passive present tense for your verbs to talk about what happens.

2. You will be using **sequencers**. Sequencers are words telling us about "when" or "how long" or "how often". For example, these kinds of words are sequencers:

<u>First</u>, you do something; <u>then</u>, you do something else; <u>next</u>, you do something; <u>before</u> you do something else, you do something *(<u>before</u> I boil the water, I open the tea bag/ I boil the water <u>until</u> the chicken is ready…)*

What about the words like "repeatedly", or "twice", or "several time"? These words tell us that we are doing something more than once. So you might have sequencers that tell you "when" like *first, next, then, finally*…or sequencers tell you about "how long" such as "until/before" or words that tell you "how often" like *repeatedly, several times, twice*. This is used to tell you several things about time.

3. Finish the purpose by using non-defining relative clauses. These are <u>used to add extra information</u> about whatever you want to tell. In this case, the extra information <u>will be the purpose</u>, tell us about "why" for example, *why are we melting the chocolate?, why are we crushing the rocks?*. …<u>which</u> kills the bacteria, or….<u>which</u> prepares the tea.

Try to use more academic words to talk about a reason for something like *"<u>in order to</u> kill the bacteria"*, or *"<u>so as to</u> kill the bacteria"*, or *"<u>to make sure/ to ensure</u> the bacteria is killed"*.

We can use non-defining relative clauses to show <u>where</u> something is. For example *"next, the milk is sent to the factory, <u>where</u> it will be turned into the cheese and ice cream"*

These are very useful, I want you to know that the process report contains something similar to the main point. Give the summary of what other steps are. That only can work if you give a brief list of steps. Don't give a big list of steps.

The grammar is easy: your sentences in man-made process should contain sequencers, passive present tense, non-defining relative clauses and indefinite purpose, so that's easy.

The tough part is the verb, you don't know how to do these things. IELTS knows that you don't know how to make chocolate...so they are going to give you all the information you need in the form of these diagrams, they are going to give you the illustration and the verbs and the words, nouns and all that information. You need to look carefully at each step and think exactly what is happening. Take the verb that they give you and put it into your own word. Think about exactly what they are showing you. Think about some logic, use logic *"why do we heat things? – to melt, to cook, to warm"* Look at all these steps, make sure that you take notes on each step and give your own ideas about what is happening, the verbs and why it is happening.

PARAPHRASING:

Paraphrase the main things in the process:

Ice cream = frozen yogurt

Fruit is picked by hand = fruit is manually collected

Manually collected = collected by hand

Fruit quality checking = the fruit is checked for quality = the fruit is checked to ensure it's free of bruises and not rotten.

PROCESS SAMPLE

The diagram illustrates the process that is used to manufacture bricks for the building industry.

Summarize the information by selecting and reporting the main features and make comparisons where relevant.

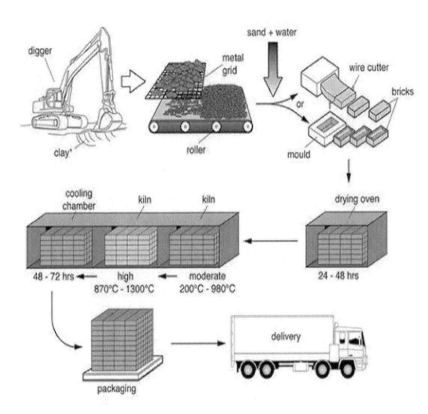

The flow chart shows the way in which bricks are made for the building industry.

Overall, there are 7 stages in the whole brick producing process, <u>beginning with</u> the digging up of clay <u>and ending with</u> the delivery of the bricks to the customers.

To begin, the clay used to make the bricks is dug up from the ground by a large digger. This clay is then placed onto a metal grid, <u>which is used to</u> break up the clay into smaller pieces. A roller assists in this process. Following this, sand and water are added to the clay, and this mixture is turned into bricks by either placing it into a mould or using a wire cut. Next, these bricks are placed in a drying oven to dry for 24 – 48 hours.

In the subsequent stage, the bricks go through a heating and cooling process. They are heated in a kiln at a moderate and then a high temperature (ranging from 200c to 1300c), followed by a cooling process in a cooling chamber for 48 – 72 hours. Finally, the bricks are packed and delivered to their destinations.

(188 words).

NATURAL PROCESS

This type of process relates to nature. This may come up in the exam, life cycle, water cycle, an animal, a plant. You might have to describe something related to the climate, weather pattern…

Natural process: one of the things about natural process that makes it challenging is they do expect you to have some basic science knowledge about these natural processes, they do expect that a natural process that you understand.

In the man-made process you can talk about the beginning and the end (the 1st step, the 2nd step, the final step). However, most natural processes are typically a cycle. So, if you are describing a natural process, you **will not** say *the 1st step…2nd step…* you should figure out which place to start. Natural processes usually use active voice, **not** ~~passive voice~~ because people are not usually involved in the natural process, so actions are not being done by somebody. It could be used passive tense sometimes for example *"clouds are flown by the winds"*, but most of the time we use active tense for natural processes.

We use the non-defining relative clauses, sequencers (instead of using *the first step, the second step, next and then,*…we might use structures like *gradually, overtime, eventually*, other things related to process time such as, *overtime, the plants grow…eventually, it produces…*)

In terms of the purpose, we might use indefinite purpose *"in order to, so as to…"* but not often because in nature, it's difficult to say why something happens.

An introduction **contains** two pieces of information: a paraphrase of the summary and the main point.

The summary is what they give you in the diagram. The summary tells you what you are looking at. You paraphrase the question and you are changing the words.

What is the purpose of the main point?

It tells you something specific about the diagram, but it does not tell you about something so specific like *"snow moves down the mountain sides.."*

If you don't know anything about the water cycle, it's quite difficult for you to do the reports natural process.

What is the purpose of the introduction?

It tells the readers this is what we are talking about, and this is something we can expect to give details in the coming paragraphs.

Task 1 writing whether that is a map, a pie chart, a man-made process, a natural process, it doesn't matter. In task 1 writing, you need to write "the main points". If you don't give the main points in your report, you will not get a band score higher than 5.0 even your vocabulary and grammar are perfect in task achievement; and really, it's quite easy for you to get a 6.0 or even 7.0 if you give the main points in your report.

Two body paragraphs

Writing 2 separate body paragraphs detailing each stage of the natural process.

NATURAL PROCESS LANGUAGE

SEQUENCERS

- Gradually,
- In order to,
- As a result of this,
- Having completed all of these steps,
- The step after this,
- The final stage of the cycle is when,
- At this point in the cycle,
- Overtime,

ORDERING

- The first stage is when + noun + verb
- To begin with
- The process commences with

MIDDLE STAGES

- Eventually,
- This step involves verb-ing
- After this stage is complete,
- The next step is when + noun + verb
- By this stage,
- The step after this + verb
- At the same time,
- While/as
- Once A has finished, B is able to start

LAST STAGE

- Once the final stage has been completed,

EXPRESSING PURPOSE

- A is done (so as) to produce B
- A is done so that/in order that B can be produced

EXPRESSING CAUSE AND RESULT

- As a result,
- This results in + noun
- A results from B/in B
- A happens, which results in B
- A happens, which leads to B
- A happens, which causes B
- A happens, with the result that B happens

Life Cycle of a Frog

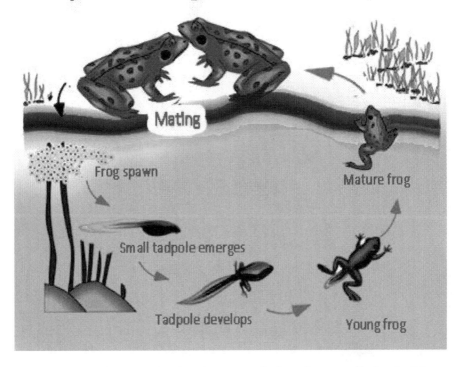

The flow chart illustrates the development of a frog from egg during its life cycle.

Overall, it is clear that there are six distinct stages illustrated in the process, commencing with producing eggs in the water and ending with the development of a mature frog.

The first stage is when the eggs, shown as frogspawn, float on the surface of the lake. The next step after this is the emergence of the small tadpole after the frogspawn hatches. At this point in the cycle, the small tadpole has a small body with a long tail. Over time, the tadpole grows and its body becomes bigger while the tail becomes longer. At the same time, the legs begin to form so as to prepare the tadpole's future life on land. Eventually, the tadpole starts to grow into a young frog with a wider mouth, a shorter tail and larger legs although it continues to live in the water. Gradually, the frog becomes mature, ready to leave the water and moves onto the land. When being on land, it starts to breathe air and loses the tail. The final stage of the cycle is when the adult frog finds a mate in order to lay eggs. Having completed all these steps, the lifecycle will then begin again.

(215 words)

IELTS WRITING TASK 2 INTRODUCTION

In task 2 writing, you have to write 250 words minimum. If you write fewer than 250 words, you will lower your score because you will <u>not explain your ideas very well</u>. You should need to be a super hero, try to produce a lot of good words. If you write 340 words, you are <u>not being organized</u>. Also, the longer your essay is, the more grammar mistakes you might make, and the less time you have to write your task 1 writing, and what easier for the examiner to follow and read? A shorter essay or longer essay? Of course, the shorter essay will make them easier to follow. There is no benefit to write supper long essays. Task 2 writing is worth 2/3 your overall score, and you spend 40 minutes on it.

In task 2 writing, we will **focus on 4 types** here:

The <u>four most common types</u> are argument, thesis led, problem solution essays, two-part questions essay. The language and organization are super important, just like task 1 writing. The **organization** is huge for task 1 and task 2. In task 1, I gave you the language that you need, I gave you the grammar that you need. The language and grammar you need for task 1 writing are relatively short; and for the ideas, you don't need any ideas for task 1 writing. Everything is available from graphs or diagrams. **Task 2 is different**, the language and grammar you need for task 2 writing are more complicated. The big thing here is to pay attention to the sentence structure (concession & contrast; cause and effect statements; this may lead to, as a result...), pay attention to the structures that you've learned for task 1 writing, because you will use a lot of those structures for task 2 writing. What the big deal here? The big deal is that the overall thing you need to understand is "every sentence has its own purpose". These are going to the engineer of your piece of writing. You need to plan them, you need to make sure every piece fits together, and everything is close. You can still get a high score if you make grammar mistakes. Try to be clear, be organized, be concise, and write at least 250 words, and done.

MOST COMMON MISTAKES STUDENTS MAKE IN IELTS WRITING TASK 2

1. Do not use (...) (etc) when writing a list. Instead, lists of examples should follow the pattern; (A and B), (A, B, and C), or (A, B, C, and D). For example: *one of the biggest problems in big cities is unemployment, crime and pollution.*

2. No question mark in your essay: Do **not** ask the reader any **questions** in your essays. For example; *"How do you think we can solve the problem of over-crowding in cities?"*

3. Do not use **exclamation points** in your essays. Don't yell at the reader. For example; *"In my opinion, it's the best solution to over-crowding in cities!"*

4. Phrases like **"more and more", "bigger and bigger", "greater and greater"** are too informal, and only good for speaking, not good for academic writing. Instead of writing *"more and more people are driving cars these days"*, you could use trend language in task 1 writing to write this sentence like *"increasing numbers of people are using cars these days" "a significantly larger number of people using cars these days" "a growing increase in the number of people using cars these days", "nowadays, the number of people who own cars has increased"; "increasing numbers of students are going abroad for university study"; "the number of cities that suffer from pollution has increased tremendously in recent decades".* That's much better than **"more and more"**. In addition, instead of using the structure such as **"much more",** you can say **"a great deal larger".** Also, **"big"** is too informal for reports and essays, we should use **"large" "sizeable" "significant"** instead.

5. Do not begin sentences with **"And", "But", "Or".** Instead use linking phrases that sound more academic such as **"In addition/Furthermore", "However", "Since", "As a result".**

6. The first sentence of each body paragraph should be a topic sentence, it should define the content of the paragraph in general terms. The number one job of the topic sentence is to tell the readers what they are going to read in that paragraph. It's a signal to the readers. A topic sentence can do other things, but its number one job is to send the signal to the readers.

7. **"Most/almost"**: **"Most"** is an adjective (usually) which means the greatest quantity, amount, measure, degree or number of something. It is followed by a noun, prepositional phrase or adjective: "Most people", "the most popular" "most of his time", "most of my friends study abroad".

"Almost" is an adverb which means **very nearly** (a language of estimation), it means **close**, but NOT totally. Examples: "We're almost home.", "almost finished", "almost every house", "almost never" "almost all of the students".

8. **Manage your time well**. **Task 1= 20 minutes. Task 2=40 minutes**. A poorly written essay for the report will receive a higher band score than an incomplete one. **Task 1 = 150 words, Task 2 = 250 words**. Make sure you write the minimum number of words.

9. **Subject-verb agreement**: He, she, it....plays, does, receives, negotiates, etc. This is a rule you learned in elementary grammar. You cannot still be making this mistake on the IELTS test. If you make this mistake in your essay, you can forget about getting a good band score.

10. **Use the correct verb tenses**. This is another elementary mistake that will keep you from getting a good band score. Pay attention to every verb you write and consider what tense you should be using. Particularly, present tense. Most of the time, the vast majority, the overwhelming majority of the time, you are using the present tense. I would say that really no need for past tense, maybe some future, maybe modal verbs, but most of the time, you are using the present tense (present simple, present perfect, present continuous). That's what something you should be thinking about.

11. **Articles** (a, an, the, no article): The last of the three biggest elementary mistakes. Maybe because you have articles in your own language. It's a foreign concept to you. The other thing is you don't read them out, and you usually use articles in theories whereas the best way on how to use articles is by looking at a lot of proper accurate writings. Review the rules about articles and apply them to every noun you write.

12. **Singular/Plural, Countable/Uncountable**: When speaking in general

about something, use the plural form. For example: "**People** use **computers** in their offices every day. (Don't say: people use ~~a computer~~ in their ~~office~~ every day); or: people need a lot of money for their **lives** (don't say: people need a lot of money for their ~~life.~~)

When it comes to Countable & Uncountable, it's a bit challenging here because there aren't rules what is countable and what is uncountable. I would say keep a little list of words that are countable and uncountable. I don't want to see ~~equipments, knowledges, advises, informations~~, etc. these are common mistakes students make.

13. In essays, **no personal opinions** in the body paragraphs (**NO** ~~I think, I believe, in my mind, in my opinion, as far as I am concerned, for me, to me,~~ etc.), only in the introduction (for thesis-led) or conclusion. Use **impersonal opinions** in the body paragraphs such as "some people think, other people believe, many people claim that, as far as some people are concerned". Try to give other people's opinions, **not** your opinion in your body paragraphs.

14. Write your essays from a **global perspective**, because the questions are asked from a global perspective. Try to avoid relating the essay question only to your country. It should be about the world in general. If you say *"traffic in the city is a serious problem when you are traveling down <u>Madison Avenue</u> at rush hour"*, it's very specific. Instead, you should say: *"when people travel down <u>busy streets in urban areas</u> during rush hours…"* now you are not talking about problems of a specific city, you are talking about <u>problems that every city faces</u>. That's what you want. You want to be general.

15. Use **linking words and transition phrases** at the beginning of all body paragraphs, and the conclusion. Keep your sentences short and well linked. It's a key if you want to improve your grammar. It will help your grammar and your organization as well. For example: *Firstly, on the one hand, on the other hand, in summary.*

16. No contractions; for example: *"shouldn't" = should not, can't = cannot, wouldn't = would not, shouldn't = should not, etc.*

17. Keep pronouns out of the essay body paragraphs. Words such as, you, we, I, us, <u>should be omitted or written as</u> people, students, society, etc.

For example, instead of saying "when ~~you~~ go abroad, ~~you~~ will have a chance to experience new cultures", you should say "when a student goes abroad, they will have a chance to experience new cultures"

18. Active tense <u>can be changed to</u> **passive tense** to omit the pronoun.

19. Effect is a noun. **Affect** is a verb.

20. In the introduction, do not tell the reader what you're going to do. For example: *"~~In this essay I will discuss the advantages and disadvantages of studying abroad~~"*. No need. The way that I will teach you how to give an introduction is going to be incredibly clear, and incredibly high level. I'm not just teaching you how to write essays for a 5.5 in the exam, I'm teaching you how to write essays that will be good for any university in the world. So, my method is incredibly clear, but helps you with your organization. So, instead you could write a concise thesis statement like *"This essay will show both the positive and negative benefits of studying abroad"*.

21. Avoid using absolutes such as; *all, every, none, only, always, never, completely, totally*. For example: when ~~everyone~~ goes abroad, they ~~always~~ suffer home sickness. Be careful of using 100% and 0% statements.

22. Don't use the word **"thing"** <u>to name the object or action you're writing about</u>. For example, instead of writing *"when students go abroad, they have opportunities to experience many different ~~things~~"*, you should write *"when students go abroad, they have opportunities to experience many different things, such as new cultures and make new friends"*. That's ok, because you are giving two specific examples about what things you are talking about.

Review this list. When you've done with your first essay, go through the list to make sure you are not making some of these mistakes.

THE LIST OF IMPERSONAL OPINION

- It cannot be denied that: *It cannot be denied that money plays an important role in people's lives.*
- It is often claimed: *It is often claimed that money cannot buy happiness.*
- People often claim that: *People often claim that children cannot grow up perfectly without a parental present.*
- Some people argue that: *Some people argue that it is more important to have an enjoyable job than to earn a lot of money.*
- Many argue that: *Many argue that old workers should be permitted to work even after reaching the retirement age.*
- It is true to say that: *It is true to say that the global warming is caused by pollution and other environmental damage.*
- It is undeniable: *It is undeniable that watching TV programs has both positive and negative effects on people.*

THE LIST OF PERSONAL OPINION

- In my opinion/view: *In my opinion/view, men and women should have the same educational opportunities.*
- To my mind: *To my mind, everyone should be encouraged to stay in school until 18.*
- To my way of thinking: *To my way of thinking, there are various reasons why people decide to live in big cities.*
- As far as I am concerned: *As far as I am concerned, shopping online is very convenient.*
- It seems to me that: *It seems to me that death penalty is essential to prevent human from committing serious crimes.*
- I believe that: *I believe that it is more beneficial for children to have homework.*

LANGUAGE TO INTRODUCE EXAMPLES

- For example: ... *For example, I'm going to buy a new suit for the party tonight.*

- For instance: .... *For instance, a father who has good skill in sports would have children with good skills in sports as well.*

- ...such as: *Some countries in Europe such as the UK, Italy, and France,....*

- ...namely: *Minor crimes, namely pick pocketing and traffic offenses, should not have the same penalty as serious crimes, such as manslaughter and murder.*

- ...particularly: *This course is particularly suitable for science students, particularly those in engineering.*

LANGUAGE TO ADD MORE POINTS TO THE SAME TOPIC

- What is more: ......*What is more*, *I think the most important benefit of visiting a new place is that you could develop your understanding of the world.*
- Furthermore: .... *Furthermore*, *children expect to be taken on holiday when they are off school during the summer.*
- Moreover: ..... *Moreover*, *the shortage of state budget may cause the lack of investment in upgrading schools' equipment and infrastructure.*
- In addition: ... *In addition*, TED *helps to keep people informed with the latest technology...*
- ...as well: ....*international tourism has disadvantages as well*.
- Not only...but also...: *The nicotine in cigarettes not only causes cancer but also leads to several other serious diseases.*

LANGUAGE TO MAKE CONTRASTING POINTS

- However,…: *We live in a technological age. However, technology cannot solve all the world's problems.*
- While/whereas: *Males spend 30 minutes a day doing the cooking while/ whereas females spend 65 minutes a day on this activity.*
- Nonetheless/Nevertheless: *While they don't trust each other, nonetheless/ nevertheless they have worked together for many years.*
- Though/although: *Although/though Tom has a lot of money, he lives in a small, old house.*
- In contrast/By contrast: *In contrast/ by contrast, the percentage of people who walked to/from work decreased.*
- Despite the fact that... *Despite the fact that he studied hard, he couldn't pass the test.*

LANGUAGE FOR BALANCE/CONTRASTING STATEMENTS

- While it is true to say that..., in fact/actually...: *While it is true to say that the city is noisy, dirty and overcrowded, in fact/ actually, it is a very interesting place to visit.*

LANGUAGE TO TALK ABOUT "REALITY"

- Indeed: *Indeed, traditional culture is slowly being wiped out by the strong current of technology.*
- Actually: *Actually, it's quite an old, historic town.*
- In fact: *In fact, my brother and I don't have much in common at all.*
- As a matter of fact: *As a matter of fact, exchanging gifts is not our traditional practice.*
- The fact of the matter is (that): *the fact of the matter is that the number of old workers has increased these days.*

LANGUAGE TO EMPHASIZE A POINT

- Of course: *Of course, the most effective way for you to improve your writing skill is through practice.*
- Obviously: *Obviously, this method can help people reduce stress and negative feelings.*
- Needless to say: *Needless to say the number of criminals increases in many countries nowadays.*
- Essentially: *Essentially, unemployed people need to find a way to make a living.*

LANGUAGE TO PROVIDE CAUSE OR REASON

- This is because: *A vast majority of people prefer cycling. This is because riding a bicycle to work is healthier than driving.*
- This may be caused by: ….. *This may be caused by the effects of global warming.*
- This can be explained by: *This can be explained by the fact that movies have been considered to be fashionable and entertaining.*
  This can be explained by a huge amount of homework assigned by teachers.
- The reason for this is that: *The reason for this is that happiness means different thing to different people.*

LANGUAGE TO TALK ABOUT "RESULT/EFFECT"

- Cause: *The unlimited use of cars may cause many problems.*
- May/Might lead to/result in: *Urbanization might lead to crime, traffic congestion, and pollution in cities.*
  An increase in the number of the elderly in recent years may lead to an aging population.
  Qualifications and skills may/might result in promotions.
- As a result: *As a result of tourism and the increasing number of people traveling, there is a growing demand for flights.*
- Consequently: *He forgot to pay his phone bill. Consequently, they turned off his service.*
- One result of this is that: *One result of this is that these individuals prefer driving cars rather than walking for exercise*

HOW TO MANAGE YOUR TIME IN TASK 2 WRITING

Time management is difficult but very important in the writing exam. It's quite easy to spend too long on one task, or even on one part of a single piece of writing. This certainly will lead to having serious consequence. This prevents you from finishing both 2 tasks of your writing within 60 minutes.

The best way to avoid this is to divide your time wisely and strictly as following:

Planning stage (10 mins):

a)   Read the question.
b)   Decide your overall opinion.
c)   Note down ideas: both arguments and evidence.

Writing stage (30 mins):

a)   Write the introduction. (5 mins)
b)   Write the first body paragraph. (10 mins)
c)   Write the second body paragraph. (10 mins)
d)   Write the conclusion. (5 mins)

Checking stage (5 mins):

Read through your writing. Look for mistakes and correct them.

It might seem odd if you spend so long preparing at the beginning. Instead, you should spend only 25 minutes or so writing your essay - but remember the most important stage is actually the amount of time you are going to spend on planning before writing your essay.

If you use this time wisely to generate plenty of good ideas, you will be able to write a good essay quickly. In contrast, if you start writing too early, there is a possibility that you will misunderstand the question, organize your information badly, fill your essay poorly or run out of ideas. Any of these things will definitely result in a low band score.

Remember that if you follow the timings above, you only need to write at a speed of ten words per minute to reach the minimum word count.

TASK 2 WRITING TYPES

Let's talk about the basic organization: the two most common essay types we have here. One of them is called THE ARGUMENT LED (EVIDENCE LED), and the other one is called THE THESIS LED. There are very clear differences and very clear similarities between these two types of essay. Let's talk about them.

The first rule is that they won't tell you what type of essay to write. IELTS **does not** say *"write the thesis led"*. No, they will give you a topic, and you need to decide what the best way to organize the essay. There is some flexibility there. Sometimes, you can write **the thesis led**, or write **the argument led**. It's up to you.

But, right now, let's understand the difference:

THE ARGUMENT LED (EVIDENCE LED)

I want you to think about you are a judge in a court room. What you are going to do is you are going to hear an argument between two sides. How does it work?

Well, you are going to give an introduction that contains some very clear information. First of all, your first sentence is going to introduce the topic. It is going to be a general statement, this is not having an opinion, but it is a general and true statement that tells the reader what the topic is? So you might say something like:

"Nowadays, nuclear energy is a popular way to provide electricity."

"In modern society, playing video games has become very popular for teenagers." Is that true? **YES.**

So, when you read that sentence, you know *"hey, this essay is about technology and teenagers"* it tells the readers what the essay is going to be about.

"In recent times, increasing numbers of students go abroad for university study." Is that true? **YES.**

Reading that context statement tells the reader this is what the essay is about. After you give the context to the reader, you need to introduce that there are two sides to this context. So, you could say something *like* *"nowadays, going abroad for university study is increasingly popular. Some people think this brings a lot of disadvantages. However, other people claim it brings a lot of benefits"* I just draw up a topic, and I'm bringing up that some people think this, other people think that. **No personal opinions**. If you read an essay and it gives you 2 impersonal opinions, you don't expect that it focuses on one side. You expect that it tells you *"I don't know what my opinion is. I'm looking at both sides."* If I wrote an essay that in the introduction it said *"smart phones are very popular nowadays. I think Apples make the best smart phones."* Do you think I'm spending the whole paragraph talking about how great Samsung is? **No.** When I give you a clear personal opinion, you know I've already made my decision and I'm going to talk about that decision. On the other hand, when I give you 2 impersonal opinions. When I say *"nowadays, smart phones have become very popular. Some people really like Samsung. However, a lot of people like apples."* Do I have a clear personal opinion here? **No**, you don't know what my opinion is, you don't know what I think. Therefore, I'm signaling to you that I don't know what I think. I'm going to spend my essay talking about both of these things.

So exactly that, in the introduction, you are basically giving me the context and 2 main ideas. What the first one is, and what the second one is. You are signaling what the main ideas are.

Now I expect in the **body paragraphs**. In the body paragraphs, you are going to give the reader the supporting ideas to support the main ideas, and that's exactly what you are going to do. You are going to write 2 body paragraphs. One body paragraph will be talking about the reasons for one opinion. The other body paragraph will be the reasons for the other opinion. And they will look a lot like part 3 speaking. The same structure that you use for part 3 speaking, you will use for task 2 writing.

Conclusion. What do you do? It's easy. You can certainly remind the reader of what the topic was. You can paraphrase yourself basically, you will paraphrase the sentence you wrote in the introduction. The first sentence of the introduction might look very similar, but not identical to the first sentence of your conclusion. Then you rephrase and summarize the two opinions.

Example: *"In conclusion, studying abroad is very popular these days. Some people claim that causes home sickness and it's too expensive, while other people think it creates opportunities for education and personal development."* You just told me the two main ideas from the both sides.

THE ARGUMENT LED SAMPLE

Some people believe that studying at university or college is the best route to a successful career, while others believe that it is better to get a job straight after school. Discuss both views.

MODEL ANSWER:

Right after finishing high school, teenagers often wonder whether they ought to continue their education or get a job. While many people believe that keeping on studying at a college or university will be the best way to guarantee a successful career, others claim that working straight after school is a better option.

Start working straight after graduation is beneficial for several reasons. Firstly, by working, young people will be able to start earning money as soon as possible. As a result, they will be mature enough, and be able to live independently on their own income. Secondly, a person who decides to look for a job rather than pursuing higher education is likely to have a chance to obtain a lot of real experience and practical skills. This may lead them to progress more quickly in their chosen profession.

On the other hand, some people argue that it is more beneficial for young people to continue their studies after high school. Firstly, a college education prepares students to meet academic qualifications, which most employers require nowadays. Consequently, university graduates usually have opportunities to earn higher salaries than those without qualifications. In addition, the job market is becoming increasingly competitive since hundreds of applicants often chase one position in an organization. Having a degree is an obvious advantage that university graduates have. In many countries, students who graduate with an engineering degree are highly paid and have an easy time getting a good job.

In conclusion, it is true to say that both working straight after high school and continuing higher-level studies each has their own unique advantages.

(270 words)

IELTS EXAMINER COMMENTS

+ Task response:

You wrote 270 words, which is long enough! Aim for 260-290 words to be safe. Less than 250 words will lose lots of marks. Your first paragraph paraphrases the whole question. Your points are all relevant and well supported with examples and explanations

+ Coherence and cohesion:

There is a clear overall progression in the writing and ideas are well organized. Paragraphs and sentences are very well constructed. Good topic sentences. You have used a range of linkers throughout the essay.

+ Lexical resource:

The range of vocabulary is very good and there is flexibility in use. "Good vocabulary" *guarantee a successful career, to live independently, pursuing higher education, to obtain a lot of real experience, progress rapidly, to meet academic qualifications*

+ Grammatical range and accuracy:

You use a range of structures accurately and there is a good range of structures. No errors detected.

THESIS LED ESSAY

The thesis-led essay is different. You are a lawyer, not a judge. You are not looking at both sides. You are only looking at one side. Likewise, give the reader the context of the background. The first sentence of these essays (argument led and thesis led) could look exactly the same. But where it is different in the thesis led is that we need a personal opinion. We need to know that you've already made a decision about what you think. Can you give the reader an impersonal opinion? Can you give one? Yes, you can, but you have to make sure that you will give me a personal opinion. So it is ok for you to say *"some people think going abroad brings advantages. However, I believe that it causes a lot of problems."*

Then, what do you do? Body paragraphs will be a little bit different. In an argument led, you will have 2 paragraphs. One is about advantages, the other one might be about disadvantages. If we talk about the advantages of studying abroad, we might talk about education, we can talk about new cultures, and we can talk about the chance to be more mature. You can talk all of those in one body paragraph in an argument led. However, **in a thesis led**, each one of these is going to become a supportive paragraph, a smaller paragraph but a supportive paragraph. So, a little bit different. You might see one introduction paragraph, two body paragraphs, and one conclusion paragraph.

Conclusion: rephrases, paraphrase yourself. Rephrase and summarize your points.

"In conclusion, going abroad is becoming very popular. I think it's a good idea for children to go overseas because it increases the chances of getting a better education, gain access to different cultures, and becoming more mature."

Do you need to give examples in your essay?

No need, if you are a very good writer with over 300 words in 40 minutes, you can give examples in your essay. However, if you have a hard time writing over 300 words in 40 minutes, and being accurate with your grammar, I would say that you should avoid many specific examples.

When it comes to the **introduction**. No surprise here:

"In recent decades, there has been tremendously economic development (is that true? YES). However, the gap between the rich and the poor nations remains considerable (is that true? YES)."

What structure am I using here? Concession & contrast

It's true that people make more money. However, there are still a lot of poor people in the world. So I'm saying something is true; however, something else is true.

You can use concession & contrast in <u>your introduction</u>, your <u>body paragraphs</u> as well as in your <u>conclusion</u>, you can use it everywhere.

Don't try to show the reader <u>how smart you are</u>. **Don't** <u>write like a writer</u>. Try to be clear.

Why should you use might, may, could, can?

<u>To show something that can happen</u>. **Don't** make a statement sound like **100% or 0%**, show that things are possible by saying *"maybe it could/ maybe it can."*

A system of a wealthy nation <u>could be</u> very beneficial……. because it <u>may be</u> the best chance to develop.

The first sentence of each paragraph, we **should** tell the reader what the topic is; tell the reader what you think about the topic.

Keep your ideas <u>short</u>, <u>clear</u> and <u>well linked</u>, and <u>well signal</u> "because, for instance, moreover" it helps everyone understand your writing.

THESIS-LED ESSAY STRUCTURE

Remember there is no big difference between thesis-led and argument-led.

The only difference is the organization and where the information is. The first paragraph will be obviously the introduction.

INTRODUCTION:

What do we want to have in the introduction?

The context: **Personal opinion** usually be written following the impersonal opinions

BODY PARAGRAPHS: no personal opinion in the body paragraph

- Body paragraph 1: 2-3 points
- Body paragraph 2: 2-3 points

CONCLUSION:

Restate the context in the introduction.

THESIS-LED SAMPLE

Some people say that what children watch influences their behavior. Others believe the amount of time they spend on television influences their behavior most.

Discuss both views and give your opinion.

MODEL ESSAY:

While it is true that watching TV affects children, it is difficult to determine whether it is the content of the programs or the length of time spent watching them that has a more significant impact on children. It seems to me that although the amount of time does affect youngsters, it is the content of the programs that has a more marked influence on them.

On the one hand, the consequences of watching TV for long periods of time can be deleterious. Firstly, the longer children are exposed to TV programs, the more likely it is for them to become addicted to watching television. When children become over-reliant on television for entertainment, they might neglect engagement in outdoor activities. This may result in a sedentary lifestyle that is highly detrimental to their physical health. More importantly, excessive TV watching impairs children's communication abilities, so they find it hard to play or live in harmony with others. As a result, children would feel discouraged from having real interactions with people around them if they spent a huge amount of time in front of the screen, which may hinder their development of social skills.

On the other hand, it is the broadcasted images that have the most direct effects on young viewers. Firstly, in most countries the majority of TV shows present glamorized depictions of inappropriate materials such as violence, drug abuse or casual sex, thus youngsters may adopt unhealthy habits and improper behavior. For example, they might fall under the impression that the use of alcoholic drinks is fashionable without being aware of the health risks they carry and later end up consuming these substances. Besides, in our modern consumer society, commercials also affect how children behave. Unwary young viewers could be easily swayed by captivating advertisements for junk food or video games, products whose target audience includes children, and so may pester their parents to buy these goods impulsively.

In conclusion, although both factors have their own implications, I believe the element with more considerable impacts on children is the content. Hence, parental involvement is essential in controlling children's TV viewing habits and in shaping a child's values to help them enter adult life with a healthy mind.

360 words

IELTS EXAMINER COMMENTS

+ Task response:

This was an interesting task question, and you answered the question fully. I cannot improve on the technique which you used. You stated your position clearly in the introduction and consistently throughout the essay. The beginning of paragraph 3 and your conclusion were the ideal places to restate your opinion. All the points which you mentioned were relevant and fully developed and I have to give a score of 8.5 for this section.

+ Coherence and cohesion:

Your paragraph structure was, as I have already mentioned, clear and logical. I then looked at your topic sentences. These indicated expertly the central idea in each paragraph. I, therefore, scored 9

+ Lexical resource:

The language meets the criteria (natural and appropriate). The essay contained some good topic vocabulary: become addicted to watching television, become over-reliant on television for entertainment, engagement in outdoor activities, find it hard to play or live in harmony with others, feel discouraged from having real interactions, etc.

+ Grammatical range and accuracy:

You certainly used a good range of grammar, including adverb clauses, relative clauses, conditional forms, comparatives and other useful constructions. So, this section again achieves a maximum score.

SAMPLE 2

Some people believe that people have the right to university education, and government should make it free no matter what their financial background. To what extent do you agree or disagree?

MODEL ESSAY:

It is true that some people argue for the universal right to free university education. While I accept that this may suit many people, I believe that it is impractical for governments to implement such a policy.

On the one hand, it is not a practical dream to expect government authorities to fund higher education for those poorer sections of society, with low incomes and no savings. Without such funding, people from poor backgrounds would be unable to attend university. As a result, they would be excluded from many well-paid careers as engineers, doctors or lawyers. Social inequalities would be perpetuated and society as a whole would suffer, since those from low-income backgrounds would have no opportunity to develop their talents. The example of the US, during the struggle for civil rights for blacks and other minorities, shows the folly of denying equal educational opportunities for the poor.

On the other hand, there would be an enormous strain on government budgets if free access to university were a right for everyone. At its simplest, people from rich families can afford to pay tuition fees and for their own maintenance during their studies. Attendance at university is a privilege, not a right, and if students can afford to pay for their studies, they should do so. In practical terms, governments cannot pay for the rich as well as the poor. Governments are faced with practical decisions on how to allocate their finite budgets, and funding free higher education for everyone would mean less money to spend on pressing issues such as health care or the environment.

In conclusion, I disagree with the view that free higher education should be a right for everyone in society, and funding should be limited to those who otherwise could not afford to attend university.

297 words

SAMPLE 3

Schools should not force children to learn a foreign language. To what extent do you agree with this statement?

MODEL ESSAY:

It is true that some people argue that a foreign language should not be one of the compulsory subjects studied in schools. While I believe that it is useful for schoolchildren to learn a foreign language, I completely agree that they should not be forced to do so.

On the one hand, it will benefit the education of most children if they are encouraged to learn a foreign language during their school years. Firstly, through studying the language they will learn about the culture of that country, and some schools even arrange exchange visits, to enable students to briefly immerse themselves in the culture of the foreign country whose language they are learning. Secondly, children can access information in another language. For example, if they are studying English, they can enjoy websites which are only available in English on any topic in which they are interested. Finally, children can be encouraged to learn a foreign language through the range of enjoyable and fun materials available nowadays, especially interactive online learning.

On the other hand, it would be counterproductive to forcibly oblige schoolchildren to learn a foreign language. One reason is that children will not learn effectively through compulsion alone. They must be motivated to do so and this is only achieved through enthusiastic teachers who select stimulating language-learning activities. Another reason is that schoolchildren will be reluctant to learn a foreign language if they cannot see why it might be relevant to their present or future lives. For example, individual Vietnamese pupils should not be forced to learn English if they are certain that they will never need or want to use it in the future.

In conclusion, I would argue that schools should encourage, but not compel, children to learn a foreign language.

292 words

ADVANTAGES AND DISADVANTAGES ESSAY

You might also see a question in the exam that asks you to discuss the advantages and/or disadvantages of a topic. For example:

- *People in the community can buy cheaper products nowadays. Do the advantages outweigh the disadvantages?*
- *New technologies have changed the way children spend their free time. Do the advantages outweigh the disadvantages?*
- *In many countries nowadays, young single people no longer stay with their parents until they are married, but leave to study or work somewhere else. Do you think this trend has more advantages or disadvantages?*

ADVANTAGES AND DISADVANTAGES ESSAY STRUCTURE

INTRODUCTION:

Introduce the topic of the essay

Say what the discussion is about (i.e. what the two different sides believe (advantages and disadvantages)   )

BODY PARAGRAPH 1 (2-3 Advantages):

A topic sentence to say what the paragraph is about

Argument 1

Evidence 1

Argument 2

Evidence 2

BODY PARAGRAPH 2 (2-3 Disadvantages):

A topic sentence to say what the paragraph is about

Argument 1

Evidence 1

Argument 2

Evidence 2

CONCLUSION:

Summarise key arguments (paraphrasing them)

Your conclusion should contain no new information.

Note:

Arguments are introduced by using impersonal opinions.

Evidence can include examples, explanations, facts or consequences. When giving evidence, it is often helpful to start general, then go more specific.

ADVANTAGES AND DISADVANTAGES SAMPLE

International travel has many advantages to both travelers and the country that they visited. Do Advantages outweigh the disadvantages?

MODEL ANSWER:

It is true that the growth of the international travel industry has brought many benefits to both travelers and the host nations which receive them. While there are serious negative consequences of this development, I would argue that these are outweighed by the advantages.

On the one hand, there are some aspects of international travel. Principally the tourist trade, which raises cause for concern. In terms of the tourists themselves, they often arrive at an overseas destination only to find that the prices of everything are grossly inflated. They may be overcharged for everything from a taxi, a meal in a restaurant or buying a souvenir. In terms of the host country, the problems of waste disposal, pollution and unregulated construction of hotels and tourist attractions often result in permanent damage to the environment. Many beach resorts in Thailand and Malaysia, for example, have become "concrete jungles" of high-rise hotels and apartments to accommodate mass tourism from Europe.

On the other hand, despite such grave issues, these are not insurmountable and must be considered against the advantages of the growing international travel industry. Firstly, there is ever-greater competition among tour operators to provide value for money holidays, so that holiday-makers can enjoy their experience of a foreign country and culture to the full. Secondly, the influx of foreign tourists brings money to the host country through the provision of jobs and services for the developing hotel and construction industries. Employees in these sectors generally benefit from higher wages and improved living standards.

In conclusion, I believe that the advantages of international travel for both travelers and host countries are greater than the drawbacks, serious though these are.

277 words

2 PART QUESTION ESSAY

Money is important to most people's lives (fact)

They will ask you 2 specific questions based on that topic. When it comes to organization, your answer must include the introduction, and your introduction will have at least three pieces of information in it.

INTRODUCTION: tell the reader what you are writing about. You are going to answer:

Question 1: you need to give your personal opinion in the introduction.

Question 2: you need to give your personal opinion in the introduction.

BODY 1: Answer questions 1 in detail

BODY 2: Answer questions 2 in detail

CONCLUSION: Repeat the opinion given in the introduction.

2 PART QUESTION SAMPLE

In many countries, more and more people choose to buy imported food rather than food produced locally. Why do people buy imported food? What could be done to encourage people to buy local food?

MODEL ANSWER:

It is true that the consumption of imported food has increased in recent years. There are some factors which help to account for this trend, but measures can be implemented to encourage more people to eat food which is grown locally.

In many countries, people are buying more imported food and there are a number of reasons to explain why this is happening. Firstly, the attractive marketing and presentation of imported food products give them an appealing and appetizing appearance. Consumers then come to expect certain high standards of packaging, so that food looks tasty, safe, hygienic and, in the case of some products, easy to prepare. Secondly, the availability of a wide range of imported food enables people to vary their diet and experiment with new recipes. This may provide a welcome change from eating the same meals every day, which inevitably becomes tedious and no longer stimulates the taste buds.

It is possible, however, to take steps to encourage the consumption of locally produced food. Local growers should ensure that their products always look clean and fresh. In Vietnam, for example, all the fruit and vegetables, meat and fish on display at local markets must be presented in scrupulously hygienic conditions, protected by plastic wrapping to keep away dust or flies. The government should enforce strict food safety regulations. Another measure could be to increase the variety of food produced by local farmers, which would then eliminate the need to import those foods from other countries. This would stimulate the local economy and reduce the environmental costs of transportation known as food miles.

In conclusion, while are some obvious reasons to explain the rise in popularity of imported food, some simple measures should be adopted by local food growers to meet this challenge.

294 words

SAMPLE 2:

Today, more people are traveling than ever before. Why is this the case? What are the benefits of traveling for the traveler?

MODEL ESSAY:

It is true that in many countries the number of people traveling has increased over recent years. There are reasons which can be identified to account for this trend and travelers undoubtedly benefit from the chance to travel more frequently and to visit even the most far-flung destinations.

At least two important factors help to explain why an increasing number of people are now able to enjoy domestic and international travel. Firstly, growing prosperity and a rise in living standards in many countries have enabled people to enjoy things which they could never have before. With greater disposable income, family luxuries such as holidays have now become affordable. Secondly, competition among tour operators has reduced the cost of traveling. Only a few decades ago, for example, budget airlines did not exist, but now they are used by millions of passengers each year.

In my view, in the case of both domestic and international travel, there are clear advantages for travelers. People now have a wide choice of places to go and things to see and do. They are now able to experience other parts of their own countries or to enjoy the richness of unfamiliar and, sometimes, exotic destinations. Thailand, for instance, is immensely popular with tourists from all over the world, including Vietnam. Visitors enjoy not only the unique cuisine but also the rich historical heritage of Thai temples and traditions. Another advantage for many people, now that travel is less costly, is the chance to be reunited with family members who have moved abroad because of work, study or simply in search of a better life. Family ties can be maintained and strengthened thanks to the greater opportunities to travel.

In conclusion, there are clear reasons why more people are traveling and there are obvious advantages for travelers.

299 words

IELTS EXAMINER COMMENTS

+ Task response:

This is an excellent essay with a lot of strong points. It is a very interesting one. In paragraph 2, you suggested two very relevant reasons for this trend. You explained both of them fully and you supported your second point with an example. In paragraph 3, you focused exclusively on positive impacts. You argued both point convincingly and at length, again giving real-life examples to support your ideas. My score for task response is 9

+ Coherence and cohesion:

The topic sentences were ideal. You identified your arguments perfectly in paragraph 2 and paragraph 3. As your sentences were also linked very smoothly, and for coherence/cohesion, my score is 9.

+ Lexical resource:

I think that one of the strong points is this essay is your awareness of words which combine together well ("collocations"): far-flung destinations, have a wide choice of places to go, to be immensely popular with, etc.

+ Grammatical range and accuracy:

You use a range of structures both simple and complex. As with lexis, this area of your writing is strong.

PROBLEM & SOLUTION ESSAY

Let's talk about problem & solution essay

The language that we use for part 3 speaking is really the same as the language we use for the essay (cause and effect, comparison, conditionals…)

INTRODUCTION:

Your first sentence is going to be a context. There are two ways you can do this:

You can present the problem and the context *(nowadays, traffic in cities is becoming a serious problem…/ nowadays/in recent times, the number of vehicles in cities has increased tremendously (context). As a result, the pollution from these vehicles is causing a serious problem. This problem is leading to respiratory illness for urban residents and visitors.)*

If you tell the reader your introduction, you will bring up a problem (the reader will expect that you will be <u>explaining the problem</u>, and then they need you to <u>give some solutions to solve the problem.</u>)

Using conditionals:

- If A…., then B… *(If the government invest in public transportation, then pollution level will decline…)*
- B….if A *(pollution level will decline if the government invest in public transportation.)*
- Unless A….not B *(unless governments invest in public transportation, there won't be a reduction in pollution).*
- Not A…unless B *(there won't be a reduction in pollution unless governments invest in public transportation.)*

BODY PARAGRAPHS:

1st STRUCTURE:

BODY 1:

Problem 1 + Problem 2

BODY 1:

Solution 1 + Solution 2

2nd STRUCTURE:

BODY 1:

Problem 1 + Solution 1

BODY 2:

Problem 2 + Solution 2

CONCLUSION:

Give the context, summarize what the problem is? And what the solutions are?

If you want or if you have time, you can make a prediction.

So in your conclusion, you are very much going to be repeating what you said in the introduction *(remind the reader of the problem; remind the reader of the solutions you suggested; and if you want/ if you have time, give a prediction).*

In conclusion, the large number of vehicles are reducing people's mental and physical health. Governments should/ought to/ need to spend more money on public transportation, and people must actually use them. Unless people take the environment more seriously, and governments start investing in this problem, it's likely that we won't see any reduction in this issue. (A 4-sentence conclusion: a context + problem + solution + prediction).

PROBLEM & SOLUTION SAMPLE

The gap between the rich and the poor is increasingly wide, as rich people become richer and poor people grow poorer. What problems could this situation cause? What are the solutions to address those problems?

MODEL ESSAY:

It is true that the gap between the rich and the poor is growing wider in many regions of the world. While the problems that result are complex, fundamental solutions based on expanding education should be adopted to tackle this problem.

Increasing levels of poverty and rising wealth inequalities impact on the economic growth of a country and the security of its citizens. In economic terms, the existence of a large mass of unemployed or low-paid workers directly affects domestic businesses, such as local shops and factories. As nobody has money to buy their products, they are themselves forced to close, creating further unemployment. In terms of public security, without the means of obtaining money through work, the poor may turn to crimes such as drug trafficking, prostitution, robbery and violent attacks on others. Youth unemployment has, in particular, been linked with rising crime rates.

Governments must, therefore, expand educational opportunities to benefit all their citizens, in order to reduce the gap between the rich and the poor. The provision of a better standard of schooling in slum areas of cities and in poor rural regions would enable children to reach a higher level of educational attainment. Grants and scholarships could be used to help students to remain in education for longer and gain qualifications. In particular, technical education could be expanded, helping poorer children to learn trades. In construction, engineering, and agriculture, a highly-educated workforce will be needed in the future, and skilled workers will be able to command high salaries and enjoy a decent standard of living. As work opportunities improve, crime rates will fall.

Thus, dealing with the problem at its roots, by expanding educational opportunities, the authorities would be able to reduce the gap between the wealthy and poor sectors of society.

293 words.

IELTS EXAMINER COMMENTS

+ Task response:

Certainly, this essay meets most of the criteria for a very high band score. I would characterize your response as "well-developed, with relevant, extended and supported ideas". Correctly, you did not try to discuss too many reasons for the problem [you focused on two important reasons in paragraph 2].

+ Coherence and cohesion:

As always, you provided a well-organized essay. The logical paragraph structure is supported by precise topic sentences and clearly identified arguments. Sentences were well-linked.

+ Lexical resource:

There is some excellent vocabulary too: *Increasing levels of poverty and rising wealth inequalities impact on the economic growth of a country and the security of its citizens/ the poor may turn to crimes such as drug trafficking, prostitution, robbery and violent attacks on others....*

+ Grammatical range and accuracy:

As with lexis, this area of your writing is strong. There is no problem with the range of grammar structures, which included a second conditional sentence, relative clauses and the consistently correct use of modal auxiliary verbs

TASK 2 WRITING LANGUAGE

CAUTIOUS LANGUAGE

When do we use "therefore"? When we use cause and effect.

For example: *it's very cold. Therefore, I put my jacket on.*

The ticket was very expensive. Therefore/so, I had saved money for many months.

You are showing a relationship.

Something causes something else. Therefore, I think (a personal opinion)

Something that is a cause. Therefore, there is a fact.

Clear signals: *It cannot be denied that/moreover/also/meanwhile/nevertheless/I am of the opinion that.*

If you want to make a statement/claim that you are harder to prove it wrong, you need to make a weaker statement.

For example: *email may cause extra work and stress.* I'm not saying it does, because if it does, it's a fact....so be cautious.

ADVERBS OF FREQUENCY

Obviously, you can use adverbs of frequency.

If I say *"globalization is an effective mean to stimulate economic growth."* (This is a 100% statement)

Every time globalization is involved, it boosts economy. (This is a 100% statement.)

It's better if I say *"globalization is usually/frequently/often/sometimes an effective mean to stimulate economic growth."* (I am making a weaker claim, it's not a strong one. It's not a 100% statement, but it is a lot harder for you to prove me wrong).

ADVERBS OF PROBABILITY

Adverbs of probability: *Reading my book leads to an 8.0* (sounds like a promise/guarantee). It's dangerous to say something like that.

It's **much better** if you say:

Reading my book is likely to lead to an 8.0

Reading my book possibly leads to an 8.0

Reading my book perhaps leads to an 8.0

Reading my book probably leads to an 8.0

IMPERSONAL VERB FORMS

It seems…

It appears….

This just tells the reader that you are not an expert. You don't have all of the facts, but the facts that you do have make you think about this.

It appears that all Vietnamese adults ride motorbikes (NOT all Vietnamese adults ride motorbikes)

MODAL VERBS

Email can / could / may / might lead to extra work and stress (we use modal verbs to show a possibility or unclear future).

SYNONYMS FOR PARAPHRASING

- **Enough:** to be sufficient, to be adequate

- **Not enough:** to be insufficient, to be inadequate, a shortage of…, a lack of….

- **Many:** numerous, various, a variety of, large number of, a range of, an increasing number/ amount, countless

- **Things:** objects, matters, issues, sectors, items, concern

- **Big:** tremendous, significant, considerable, substantial, immense, vast, profound

- **Important:** principal, crucial, major, essential, critical, vital

- **Get:** obtain, receive, acquire, gain

- **Have:** possess, encounter, undergo, experience,

- **Give:** provide, supply, contribute, offer, present

- **Do:** participate, conduct, perform, undertake, engage to, be involved in, implement

- **More:** further, additional, added

- **Too much:** an excess of, to be excessive

- **Important people:** leading, powerful, influential, well-known, prominent, famous, supportive

CONCLUSION

Thank you again for downloading this book on *"IELTS Academic Writing Task 1 + 2: The Ultimate Guide with Practice to Get a Target Band Score of 8.0+ in 10 Minutes a Day"* and reading all the way to the end. I'm extremely grateful.

If you know of anyone else who may benefit from the useful strategies, structures, tips, task 1 + task 2 language in this book, please help me inform them of this book. I would greatly appreciate it.

Finally, if you enjoyed this book and feel that it has added value to your work and study in any way, please take a couple of minutes to share your thoughts and post a REVIEW on Amazon. Your feedback will help me to continue to write other books of IELTS topic that helps you get the best results. Furthermore, if you write a simple REVIEW with positive words for this book on Amazon, you can help hundreds or perhaps thousands of other readers who may want to improve their English writing skills sounding like a native speaker. Like you, they worked hard for every penny they spend on books. With the information and recommendation you provide, they would be more likely to take action right away. We really look forward to reading your review.

Thanks again for your support and good luck!

If you enjoy my book, please write a POSITIVE REVIEW on Amazon.

-- Rachel Mitchell --

CHECK OUT OTHER BOOKS

Go here to check out other related books that might interest you:

https://www.amazon.com/dp/B06W2P6S22

Common English Mistakes Explained With Examples: Over 600
Mistakes Almost Students Make and How to Avoid Them in Less
Than 5 Minutes A Day

https://www.amazon.com/dp/B072PXVHNZ

**Paraphrasing Strategies: 10 Simple Techniques For Effective
Paraphrasing In 5 Minutes Or Less**

https://www.amazon.com/dp/B071DFG27Q

Legal Vocabulary In Use: Master 600+ Essential Legal Terms And
Phrases Explained In 10 Minutes A Day

http://www.amazon.com/dp/B01L0FKXPU

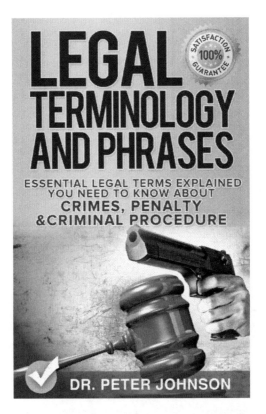

Legal Terminology And Phrases: Essential Legal Terms Explained
You Need To Know About Crimes, Penalty And Criminal Procedure

http://www.amazon.com/dp/B01L5EB54Y

Productivity Secrets For Students: The Ultimate Guide To Improve Your Mental Concentration, Kill Procrastination, Boost Memory And Maximize Productivity In Study

http://www.amazon.com/dp/B01JS52UT6

Daughter of Strife: 7 Techniques On How To Win Back Your Stubborn Teenage Daughter

https://www.amazon.com/dp/B01HS5E3V6

Parenting Teens With Love And Logic: A Survival Guide To
Overcoming The Barriers Of Adolescence About Dating, Sex And
Substance Abuse

https://www.amazon.com/dp/B01JQUTNPM

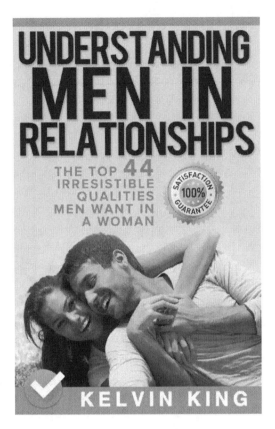

http://www.amazon.com/dp/B01K0ARNA4

Made in United States
Orlando, FL
31 May 2024

47385147R00083